CRIS ROGERS

MAKING DISCIPLES

**Elevating the conversation around
discipleship and spiritual formation**

essential
christian

awaken
MOVEMENT

Published by Essential Christian

14 Horsted Square
Uckfield
East Sussex TN22 1QG
Registered charity 1126997
www.essentialchristian.org
www.springharvest.org
www.wearemakingdisciples.com

ISBN 9781911237082

First edition 2018

Acknowledgments
Scripture quotations are taken from the Holy Bible, New International Version Anglicised. Copyright © 1979, 1984, 2011 Biblica, formerly International Bible Society. Used by permission of Hodder & Stoughton Ltd, an Hachette UK company. All rights reserved. "NIV" is a registered trademark of Biblica. UK trademark number 1448790.

A catalogue record for this book is available from the British Library

Printed and bound in the UK, February 2018, LH26

Designed by Christian Publishing & Outreach (CPO) www.cpo.org.uk

CONTENTS

[FOREWORD] ROY CROWNE

EXECUTIVE DIRECTOR, HOPE

I can still remember in my early teens, my dad referring to the three Rs as the key to me being effective in the future: the three Rs being reading, writing and arithmetic! He said these three were key to being effective in anything I wanted to do.

When you start to look at discipleship, which is one of the issues that the church is grappling with at the moment, Cris's course really captures it so well around the three Hs: heart, head, and hands.

If you were to ask me to sum up the kingdom of God, in the end it is all about relationships. The discipleship that we long to see lived out in the church, in community, is all about relationships. Chris provides a great framework for this to happen through this course and the transforming power of the gospel.

In Proverbs 4:23, we realise that our hearts are always impacted by stuff around us, which is why the writer in the book encourages us to jealously guard our hearts because from it flows the springs of life. When we understand and experience the extravagant love of God poured into our hearts, that enables us to mature as individuals and followers of Jesus.

This course will give us an ability to transform the way we see ourselves, and then in the light of that, make changes where appropriate. As we read in the book of James, the Word of God is like a mirror that reflects back at us, and some of these exercises will give us those 'aha moments' and cause us to move along in our discipleship.

It will encourage you to think, and hopefully transform your thinking on some fronts. It will provoke you, as you see your shape, to change to become a more effective follower of Jesus, knowing that we walk through this process with the Word of God and the Spirit of God transforming us.

My prayer as you go through this course is that it will cause you to take some significant steps to bring about change in your walk with God, involvement in your family, involvement in the church and being salt and light within your community.

Cris's goal is that this will be a real tool to enable us to become more like Jesus; to allow him to work in us and work through us. It is all about investing in relationships. Fruitful relationships are worth the investment we make.

The personal relationship that we have with God is truly the key to effective discipleship, and that investment within the body of Christ will bear fruit that will affect our hearts, our thinking and our actions.

So well done Cris, I prayer as you read and reflect through this book: as a church, a small group or as an individual - may it bear fruit in changed lives and actions, so the Kingdom of God will grow.

[1]
INTRODUCTION

Welcome to Making Disciples. Within these pages is an exciting new, yet richly old way of talking about discipleship and spiritual formation. All too often modern discipleship in the church is based on presumptions that are more attuned to an academic system than any biblical apprenticeship. Jesus didn't tell his disciples to listen to more of his teaching but to follow him and see how he 'did' life in relationship with God. This resource is less of a course and more of an apprenticeship framework. At the heart of Making Disciples is an assent tool helping to unlock whole life discipleship. This is then followed by a seven-week apprenticeship course aiming to unlock areas of our lives the Gospel is longing to impact. At its heart, the church has to be disciple making not just believer making. Jesus is not just looking for more believers, He is also looking for people who will give everything of themselves to His mission to change the world.

I was recently having a conversation with a friend about the Jesus Movement and what Jesus meant when He said, "go make disciples" in Matthew 28. I made her laugh when I said Jesus had believers coming out of His ears. All joking aside, Jesus has around 2.2 billion people today who claim to follow Him; that is 33 percent of the world's population. It can be argued that we are "winning" if numbers are the game. By comparison, Islam adds up to 19 percent, with the non-religious making up 12 per cent. However, it's not about having the largest group; it's about having a movement of people all living and breathing Jesus.

In reality, we are just not making the impact that we should. Jesus has believers coming out of His ears and still the church is impotent. In the children's game "Simon says", if Simon gives a command, then you have to do it. But in the church, when Jesus gives us instruction, we feel we only have to memorize it. If I asked my son to go wash the car and he came back three hours later having not done it, but only memorized what I had said, I would be disappointed. Jesus teaches us so much in the Scriptures, but rather than living it out we all too often memorize it – sometimes in the Greek.

Sadly, many people claim to be believers but Jesus never asked for more believers. Jesus talked about "disciples". In Matthew 28 Jesus sends His followers out and tells them to make more "disciples". Disciples making disciples.

There is a significant difference between believers and disciples. Believers are those who have their golden ticket. They believe Jesus lived, died, and rose again. These believers are saved and now wait for the day they die to make their way on the heaven train. This group is sitting back, attending worship, and waiting until the day they get to heaven. But there is so much more than this. God is looking for partners in His kingdom work. What God has in store for His people is much more exciting than longing and waiting for death.

In ancient Israel, a disciple was someone who followed his rabbi very closely. They wanted to see how the rabbi did life with God, how they performed the religious rituals and promoted that particular rabbi's teaching. Disciples lived in the awareness of their own smallness, and they lived in the awareness that things could be so different. They also realized that there was another world possible in the midst of this one.

In the early church, disciples followed their rabbis so strictly that it was quite difficult to know where the rabbi's life ended and the disciple's life started. The Jewish people had a phrase that encompassed this idea. If a disciple had followed their rabbi intently on the dusty roads, watching and listening closely, then at the end of the day they would be literally covered in the dust of their rabbi. So they said, "May you be covered by the dust of your rabbi."

Today, there are churches packed full of believers, but what Jesus truly wants are disciples – people who are covered in His dust. He needs people who will take seriously His direction to serve the last, the least, and the lost with their whole hearts; people who are going to see themselves as Jesus' tools in the world. The church was never meant to be an institution that contains people with religious views but a community living out Jesus. Jesus is bigger than any religion or the trappings of religion. The church is meant to be a countercultural community asking the question: what does a group of people look like in the world when they take Jesus' command to make "disciples" seriously? How would the church, before we even get to the world, be impacted if we took Jesus' radical Sermon on the Mount seriously and actually lived out His profound teaching?

Jesus never came to start a religion or an institution but a movement, a movement of people all choosing to be His disciples. Disciples who were interested in leaving simple religious beliefs behind and joining a movement of people all becoming more like Him and therefore making more disciples. The cycle was meant to go on and on.

Until we move away from simply believing, move away from religion and religious behaviour, we will never be able to live the simple life of a disciple. The questions we must ask ourselves are "What am I – a believer or a disciple?" and "What do I have in my hand to be used by Jesus? Do I hold a 'ticket' or a 'toolkit'?"

During this course, the constant reminder is that a disciple is someone who is worrying less about holding a ticket, as our salvation is guaranteed in Jesus, but wanting to invest into following and copying Jesus every day.

[”]

IF YOU SQUEEZE A LEMON
YOU GET LEMON JUICE.
IF YOU SQUEEZE A CHRISTIAN,
DO YOU GET JESUS?

ARCHBISHOP JOHN SENTAMU

[2]
GETTING STARTED

The Discipleship Shape Tool provides time and headspace to reflect upon our own discipleship. We do this by asking questions that might help us see where we need to invest and give attention. This is not a tool to leave us feeling bad or condemned but a tool that will excite us for what God has planned for us. God has more in store for us than we have at the moment. Our discipleship opens us up further to His work in and through our lives.

The heart of the church must be about making and developing disciples. This tool is about providing an opportunity to ask questions about how we are engaging and investing into each area of our lives.

Jesus was approached one day and asked, "What is the greatest commandment?" He responded, "'Love the Lord your God with all your heart and with all your soul and with all your mind and with all your strength'; and, 'Love your neighbour as yourself'" (Luke 10:27).

Love God with your heart, your soul, your mind, and your strength. Once we take this call to fully give ourselves to Christ, the Discipleship Shape Tool will give us questions to reflect upon and respond to; it teaches us to become a disciple and explores areas of potential. Personal discipleship is about moving closer to what Jesus wants for us in every area of our lives. This has been broken down into three areas – our **heads**, **hearts**, and **hands**.

At the centre of the wheel is the cross. In Mark 8:34, Jesus calls us to pick up our cross and follow Him, to walk the way of the cross. This walk is a subversive walk, a countercultural walk. This is about living a life that is giving up ourselves and laying down what is precious to us and sacrificing it for Jesus. The tool is leading us to think about moving towards Christ, dying to self, and accepting Him fully and completely.

A disciple of Jesus is called to use their mind to grow in knowledge of Him, use their hands to be active in serving Him, and to be filled with desire and passion for Him in their heart. However, many disciples can be overdeveloped in one area and underdeveloped in another.

We can end up with big heads and hearts but small hands, or big hearts but small heads and hands! Our challenge is to understand ourselves and seek to invest in areas of our lives other than our predominant area. In many areas of life it's good to play to our strengths, but when it comes to discipleship we need to be holistic and well rounded in all areas.

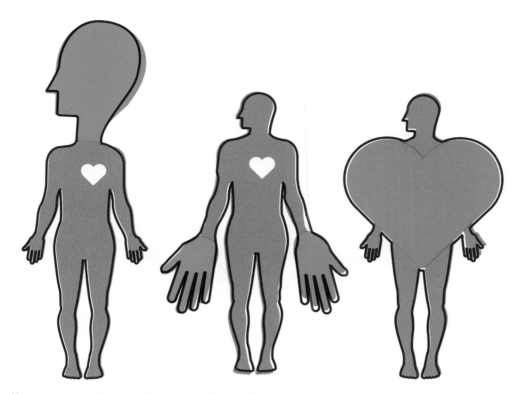

If you answer the questions honestly on the wheel (page 20) and join up the dots, you will then have a discipleship shape. The shape should indicate something of your passions and bias. For the purpose of the tool, areas near the centre are stronger and those on the edge show areas we can work on and invest. It is likely that there are one or two areas that are stronger than another. This is not a problem but an exciting opportunity. Jesus wants to transform all areas of our lives. We each have some areas in which we are stronger and more active and other areas less so.

Conversation and reflection are encouraged in conjunction with the tool. The tool can be used in a large church setting, smaller home group setting, or one-on-one with a more mature Christian you trust, or even a mentor. This person would help the user to see some ways they can develop from the areas they have identified. In an individual scale exercise the tool reveals the user's personal shape. If completed alongside a larger group, it can reveal the shape of the group or even church.

HEAD, HEART, HANDS

The key to understanding discipleship and this tool is the call to love the Lord your God with all your head, heart, and hands, which is based on the biblical foundation of Deuteronomy 6:5, to love the Lord your God with all your heart, soul, mind, and strength. Each of these areas of our lives is to be handed over to God for His rule and reign.

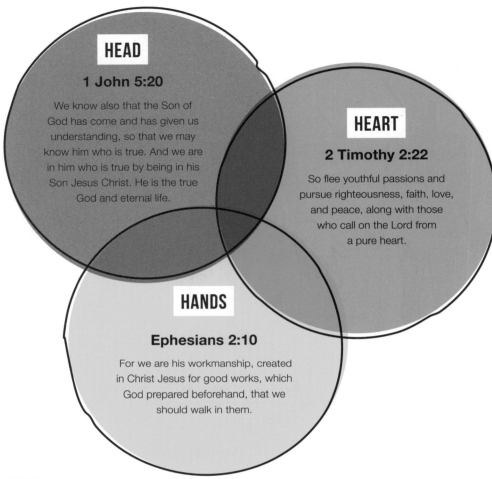

HEAD

1 John 5:20

We know also that the Son of God has come and has given us understanding, so that we may know him who is true. And we are in him who is true by being in his Son Jesus Christ. He is the true God and eternal life.

HEART

2 Timothy 2:22

So flee youthful passions and pursue righteousness, faith, love, and peace, along with those who call on the Lord from a pure heart.

HANDS

Ephesians 2:10

For we are his workmanship, created in Christ Jesus for good works, which God prepared beforehand, that we should walk in them.

HEAD

Our minds as disciples need renewing and reshaping into the mind of Christ. It is through personal reading and meditation of the Bible as well as corporate teaching, discussion with others with whom you might not agree, debating with and being challenge by others that our minds can be shaped. With the knowledge of the revelation of God's love and grace through the Spirit, our minds can become clear and effective as forgiven people.

HEART

Often, in the church, we focus on competency, but in truth is it's our character that is more important than our abilities. It is who we are in the privacy of our home that shapes everything about how we live. Your heart is where you carry your passions and desires as well as your hopes and dreams. We can talk about our hearts being aligned with the heart of Christ, who was compassionate, prayerful, broken for the poor, and sinless. It's in our hearts that we can find our dark sides and sinful nature, and it's in our pure hearts that we choose to pursue holiness, faith, love, and peace.

HANDS

The writer of James 2:14 calls us to be people who have "faith and deeds". In other words, our faith has to be accompanied by action. It's in how we serve and love others in action that our faith is revealed. Are we becoming people who serve our family, neighbourhood, and church community? Are we becoming people who give away what we have and offer our gifts in our hands to God's kingdom work? Our hands can also be used to lay on the sick, feed the hungry and point others in the right direction.

It's when these three areas of discipleship are given over to God that we find our whole lives transformed in how we think, how we feel, and what we do to embody who we are in Christ. It's in the balance of these three areas that our whole discipleship can take place.

[3] CULTURE IS KEY TO DISCIPLE MAKING

In this short section I want to explore how to create a culture of open discipleship within a church community. With the right culture this tool could radically impact not just the individual's life, but also the whole church community's life and the wider external community's life. A church culture can encourage discipleship or, alternatively, could encourage the community to be spectators driven by consumerism.

For the tool to be used well it needs to be supported by a church culture where the expectation is that everyone will play their part in the kingdom of God and used where an ethos of grace, love, openness, and encouragement is fostered. This tool hasn't been designed to bash people over the head with their weaknesses but to be a strong encourager and champion of development and growth.

Culture is created by the interplay of our beliefs, values, and practices. So, developing a discipleship culture within a local church has to be driven by a clear belief system, shared communal values, and common practices. These three things help create the foundation for discipleship. A community where people think they have to be perfect from the word go breeds a culture of projection and protectionism. Jesus wants us to only project onto others what is true and real. This kind of culture does not start with the community but is modelled by the leadership. For the Discipleship Tool to work within a community it needs to be promoted by the leadership within a healthy culture set by and lived out by the leadership.

BELIEFS

A community's central belief system will determine their behaviour. How we see God, His power, and authority will affect how we think, how we live out our faith and educate others about what is required of us as disciples. For example, if we believe the cross was sin management, then we might believe that discipleship is the activity around practising being sin-free.

A church may have many orthodox truths that are within a biblical culture, but the central belief is that of Christ's death (our salvation) and resurrection (new life in Him), meaning we have a culture of forgiveness and redemption. Jesus' death and His resurrection reveal to us His Lordship over all things. It is because of this Lordship that we recognize that Jesus is worthy of our worship and our submission; therefore, discipleship is about being people who recognize Jesus has power over our lives (submission) and power under our lives (empowerment). This means discipleship is a fundamental part of our faith development and growth.

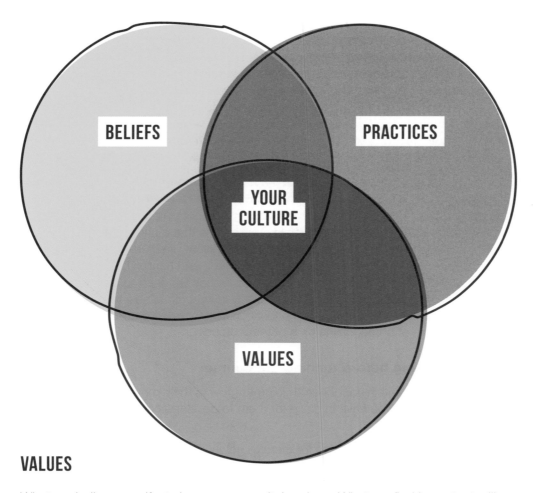

VALUES

What we believe manifests in our community's values. What we find important will be shown in the values we hold between us. For example, if we believe the gospel is only for those who deserve it or worked hard enough for it, the community will have values that manifest this. If a community has a belief that only the church leader knows best and hears from God, or is anointed to teach, then discipleship will be left to the leader to disseminate the information. But if the belief is that everyone is called to play their part within a theology of a priesthood of all believers (1 Peter 2:5), the value within the community becomes that of each member playing their part. Setting a healthy culture for disciple making only develops when the leadership holds the belief that everyone has a part to play in the life and witness of the church.

You could argue that one of the greatest barriers for the church in making disciples is that our programmes cater for consumers, not practitioners. Discipleship isn't about knowing more but about living out more deeply the life of Jesus. If our value is for each person to play their part, then discipleship becomes about individuals exploring their gifting and calling, in a safe and loving environment, so they become practitioners and not academic experts. It also becomes a key value to encourage and empower every member and not only a few.

PRACTICES

We can make discipleship so complicated people feel lost and paralysed by it. Most of what Jesus tells the disciples isn't how to do something but more the authority they have to do it. For example, when Jesus teaches the disciples to minister healing He doesn't give them a crib sheet of things to say but rather tells them they have authority to do it: "When Jesus had called the Twelve together, he gave them power and authority to drive out all demons and to cure diseases, and he sent them out to proclaim the kingdom of God and to heal the sick" (Luke 9:1–2).

In other words, disciples are people who have been authorized to carry on Jesus' kingdom work. A discipleship culture must have space for believers to see simple reproducible practices. If discipleship is following and copying Jesus, then believers need to see *what* to copy to be a disciple. This means that a church community creating a disciple-making culture must think about what practices it has in place to help someone develop in each area of head, heart, and hands. Disciples can't simply be told; we need to be developed, which means we need to be shown ways of developing. This tool will work most effectively if a church is able to connect people with avenues available within the local church to develop and signpost avenues available at home, online or in other churches.

It is worth asking before running the course:

- How is someone within your church going to grow in their knowledge (head)? What practices do you have in place for them to develop and grow in their biblical understanding?

- What opportunities do you have for them to get involved (hands) and serve both inside and outside the church? What mission opportunities can someone get involved with to grow in confidence?

- Are there ways for people to speak openly about sin and struggles and have someone mentor, support, and challenge them (heart)?

- Each church needs to be able to reinforce the basic disciplines of healthy disciples, do it in a reproducible way, and make them easy to multiply with other people.

- A well-implemented discipleship culture can take a long time to cultivate. An unhealthy culture may need significant investment to get to a healthy place. If you want a discipleship culture it has to be modelled on every level of the church community. It will involve being committed to the simple things over an extended period of time. One talk on culture will not change anything but will be a start.

Questions to think about

[Q] Are there basic foundational pieces you can implement to start to shape your church for discipleship?

[Q] If people need to be challenged, is there a support network within the church?

[Q] Do you have space in your community for more people to get involved?

[Q] Do you value each member and model a priesthood of all believers?

[Q] Do you have a variety of places where people can explore their gifts and callings?

NOTES

_____

_____

_____

_____

_____

_____

_____

_____

_____

_____

_____

_____

_____

_____

[4] HOW TO RUN THE DISCIPLE MAKING TOOL

Print out copies of the tool. For a double-sided sheet with the wheel on one side and a short unpacking of the shapes available on the other please download a copy from our website: wearemakingdisciples.com. The best way to run the tool is to explain that the tool is not about catching anyone out but about giving attention to our discipleship and encouraging reflection.

Some people can give a snap response to the questions, while others may need time to think about each answer. Each group should be given the necessary time to do this well. We encourage pencil lines so people can erase and reassess as the weeks go on.

As you go through the tool some of the questions might need further explanation. This is provided later in the book. Each question is specifically and strategically placed on the wheel to allow a strong shape to appear. If any question is not clear, do allow time to read out the longer explanation. This should not be needed for more than a couple of questions.

ASSESSING THE SHAPE

A breakdown of the shapes can be found on the following page. Most people should be able to see at least one area where they are closer to the centre, a secondary area in the middle, and then an area that is closer to the far edge. This is helpful as it means they can clearly see in which area they may want to invest.

Others may come out with more of a starfish shape. The questions are arranged to separate personal questions from questions about others. These have also been arranged to tease out questions around reflection and questions around just doing and knowing. If a user has a shape where the points are moving back and forth this would indicate an inconsistency within their life. It might be that all the points in the centre are about serving others and the points on the edge about caring for themselves. With a shape like this, the user should be encouraged to look at what the links might be between the points.

Links might be made between questions over regular daily rhythms. Some people are active and learning but not doing so regularly. Some people might connect points over being more committed to others than themselves. Others might notice a link between commitment and non-commitment.

WHAT NEXT?

The tool allows the user to assess areas within their personal discipleship in which to invest. Done as a church this can indicate the shape of the whole church. To get the best possible indication, the church would need to gather a large enough sample of the congregation.

Each week of the seven-week course will focus on one or two areas from the wheel. It is encouraged that the facilitator collect the shape sheets and hand them back each week, allowing people to reflect upon how things might be changing.

Week one of the course is simply working through the Discipleship Shape sheet. If this activity is done as a whole church, then this could be left out as you head straight into the course. If the sheet is done as a small group, then session one allows space and time to do some reflecting there and then. This could be a very helpful session to do separately, even if you have run the shape sheets at a previous gathering.

We encourage you to work through this material each week, returning to the shapes for assessment and reflection. The more people become reflective upon their shape the more they will be able to make changes they wish to see.

[5] DISCIPLE MAKING TOOL

Using a pencil, work through the questions one by one taking as much time as necessary per question. As this is a self-assessment tool, there is no right or wrong answer. Mark each answer on the line where you feel you best sit. The lines are a sliding scale from 'NOT AL ALL' through to 'SOMEWHAT' and then 'IN EVERY WAY'. Try to be as honest as possible. When you finish all the questions, join the dots to reveal your discipleship shape.

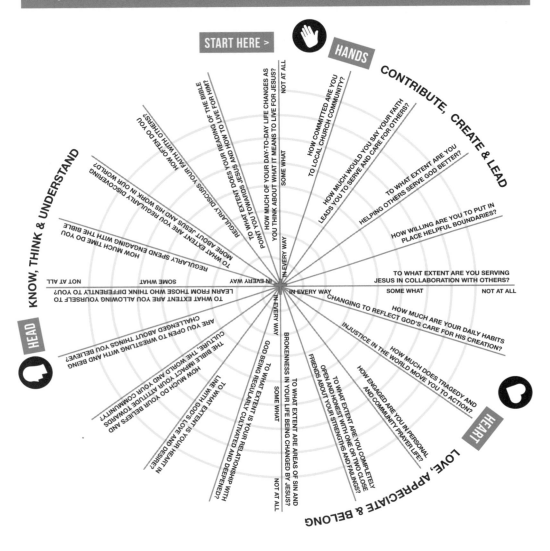

Personal discipleship is about moving closer to what Jesus wants for us in every area of our lives. We have broken that down into three areas – our heads, hearts, and hands.

A disciple of Jesus is called to use their mind (head) to grow in knowledge of Him, use their hands to be active in serving Him, and to be filled with desire and passion for Him in their heart. However, many disciples can be overdeveloped in one area and underdeveloped in another. We can end up with big heads and hearts but small hands, or big hearts but small heads and hands. Our challenge is to understand ourselves more fully and seek to invest in areas of our lives other than our predominant area.

If you have answered the questions honestly on the front page and joined up the dots you will now have a shape. The shape should indicate something of your passions and your biases. For the purpose of the tool, areas near the centre are stronger, while those on the edge show areas we can work on and invest. It is likely that you have one or two areas that are stronger than another. This is not a problem but an exciting opportunity. Jesus wants to transform all areas of our lives. We will all have some areas in which we are stronger and more active and other areas that are less so.

It may be that you would find it helpful to discuss your answers and your shape with a friend or mature Christian you trust who can help you to see some ways to strengthen those areas you have identified.

First, indicate which shape best matches your own.

The **bean** shape indicates one area being more developed than the other two. This may reveal a headstrong personality, with heart and hands that are less developed. It may also show a compassionate and active faith but lack of biblical foundations for the activity. It is easy to allow our preferred area to develop over other areas of faith. Are you able to identify your weaker areas that need the most attention?

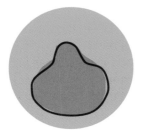

The **pear** shape shows one area out of the three that is less developed than the other two areas. It would be useful to ask yourself why this might be. Have you neglected this area or has there simply not been the opportunity to grow in it?

The **larger circle** indicates less confidence in all three areas. This is exciting, as it means there is such an adventure ahead to build up these areas to become balanced and engaged. It might be helpful to ask someone trustworthy if they agree this is a true reflection – often others see strengths that we miss!

The **pea** shape displays a rounded and balanced discipleship with head, heart, and hands working well together. The challenge here is sustainability and commitment. The more we know Christ the more we realize we don't have it all together. How do you keep developing and growing? Do you have people you are completely honest with, and do they identify any weaknesses in your growth?

The **starfish** shape is less clear. All three areas are inconsistent with themselves. This would indicate that in the head, heart, and hands there are some areas that are moving towards Jesus and others where investment is needed. It is worth flagging questions answered with "NOT AT ALL" to see if there is a link between them. Often a link between which markers are in the centre and which are on the edge can become apparent. This could be around commitment, daily rhythms, working with others, private life, and public life.

THE SPIRAL:

Did you notice the spiral in the background of the diagram? So often we make our life with Jesus like a long road we walk. We think we are always moving forwards. In reality, the same issues will resurface in our lives time and time again. Discipleship is actually more like a spiral. The question is, are we moving towards or away from Jesus? In other words, every time we hit "that old problem", are we handling things differently this time around? Are we behaving better than we did before? Are we more Christ-like this time?

DISCIPLE MAKING

Having done the Discipleship Shape Tool, each person should be able to recognize the areas that are developed and the areas in which investment is needed. Throughout the course we must keep reminding ourselves that our weaker areas in discipleship are exciting areas to grow, not areas of embarrassment. In this course, we will invest in and be challenged by one of the areas found on the tool each week – head, hands, and heart.

SESSION 0: TO BE USED WEEK 1 WITH THE TOOL

Having done the Discipleship Shape Tool with the group, here are some questions to ask:

[Q] Are you surprised by your shape?

[Q] If you had a starfish shape, is there a link between the points on the edges and the points in the middle? Can you see any consistencies or inconsistencies?

[Q] In which area do you recognize a need or wish to invest? What would it take for you to invest in this area?

[Q] Have you ever thought about taking personal responsibility for your shape as a disciple?

[Q] What could you do to invest in someone else's discipleship? Being a disciple is about making disciples. Is there someone you could help with their shape?

[Q] Who could you ask to invest in your discipleship?

PRAYER

Take some time to pray about what was revealed by the shape. If anyone is worried, then take time to name the worry and hand it over to God. If people are excited, then invite them to pray for what this means for them. Discipleship is a daily commitment in making Jesus the centre of our lives. In the prayer time you might want to take a moment to recommit lives to this adventure.

NOTES

[7]
SESSION 1: A MIND THAT IS
HOLY AND PLEASING

BIG IDEA

In Mark 8:33 Jesus turns to Peter and rebukes him with the stark words, "Get behind me, Satan!... You do not have in mind the concerns of God, but merely human concerns." Jesus wanted Peter to have a mind filled with God's concerns, not the concerns of people. Jesus wants us to offer all that we have and allow our minds to be transformed by Him. Our minds direct so much of who we are. Therefore, Jesus wants our minds to be instructed by Him and our thinking to be deepened, allowing ourselves to act more like Him.

It is possible to know about Jesus but not allow our minds to be shaped into His way of thinking. We can conform to the world's way of thinking and not allow Jesus to transform our ideas, thoughts, and views.

[Q] How fixed are your views? Do you allow others to speak into what you think about God or are you closed to views that are different from your own?

[Q] Not only can we be fixed in our views, but we can also be influenced by others. How do you allow others to shape your views?

EXTERNAL AND INTERNAL INFLUENCES

The way we see the world and our place within it is shaped by external and internal influences. It's possible to know about Jesus but not have our minds renewed by Jesus. We can believe in Jesus but have a mind conformed to this world's way of thinking. We all grow up and mature in a world that is trying to shape our view of it. Family systems and behaviours, school education, workplace culture, social and community culture, the media, newspapers, talk radio and other contexts shape our minds to think in a way that fits with the predominant culture. We also have internal influences that shape us. Our minds are always replaying old ideas and words spoken over us as children and young adults. These may not be true but they affect how we see ourselves. If you were told once you were uncoordinated, for example, you may then act that way more so. If you have been told you aren't good at sports, you may never give anything new a try. If you have been told you will not amount to much, you may allow this to shape your future. All these things are in your databanks and some of them need to be erased. You need to get a new view of God and a new view of yourself.

[Q] What external and internal influences have shaped how you see the world and your place within it?

James 1:23–24 tells us that Scripture is like a mirror that wants to give us a new way of seeing ourselves. "Anyone who listens to the word but does not do what it says is like someone who looks at his face in a mirror and, after looking at himself, goes away and immediately forgets what he looks like."

In other words, our identity must be shaped by Scripture and not the prevailing world. This takes prayer and the Holy Spirit.

PRAYER

Before reading the passage take a moment to pray. Invite the Holy Spirit to speak to the group through the passage. This is key each week. Praying before reading the Bible opens us up to God speaking and shows that we want to learn from Him as well as each other.

Therefore, I urge you, brothers and sisters, in view of God's mercy, to offer your bodies as a living sacrifice, holy and pleasing to God – this is your true and proper worship. Do not conform to the pattern of this world, but be transformed by the renewing of your mind. Then you will be able to test and approve what God's will is – his good, pleasing and perfect will.

For by the grace given me I say to every one of you: Do not think of yourself more highly than you ought, but rather think of yourself with sober judgment, in accordance with the faith God has distributed to each of you. For just as each of us has one body with many members, and these members do not all have the same function, so in Christ we, though many, form one body, and each member belongs to all the others. We have different gifts, according to the grace given to each of us. If your gift is prophesying, then prophesy in accordance with your faith; if it is serving, then serve; if it is teaching, then teach; if it is to encourage, then give encouragement; if it is giving, then give generously; if it is to lead, do it diligently; if it is to show mercy, do it cheerfully

[R] ROMANS 12:1–8

Having read the passage, pause for a moment or two. Some groups may like to read the passage twice – maybe with two different voices or from different translations.

Start by facilitating an open discussion on people's reaction to the passage, using questions like:

[Q] What jumps out of the passage for you?

[Q] Is there anything you struggle with or don't understand?

[Q] Are there any new connections you can make within or beyond this passage?

[Q] "Do not conform to the pattern of this world". The Greek here says something like "do not be bent under the influence of the world". Where do you see this in your own life?

[Q] Paul talks about our bodies being "holy and pleasing". What does it mean to have a mind that is "holy and pleasing"?

[Q] How do you know if your mind is thinking like the world or like Jesus? Are there ways for you to clarify God's ways?

[Q] This passage wants to mould our way of thinking. It wants to point out our conformed mind, challenge us to think about ourselves humbly and with sober judgment, and ponder our gifts and abilities and how to use them cheerfully. How does a passage like this make you think differently?

[Q] In the past, how has God transformed your thinking? Where do you sense He wants to transform your thinking right now?

ACTIVITY

Referring to the HEAD worksheet that follows (on page 27), ask each person to spend some time carrying out a thought audit of the mind. An easy exercise for this is to ask the participants to cast their minds back over the past twenty-four hours, or the past week, month or year. What occupies their mind? For example: thoughts about money, how others view them, justice, personal desires, etc.

Participants might ask themselves: what has been on my mind a lot?, what thoughts only pop up occasionally?, which of these ways of thinking seem to be conformed to the pattern of this world? Which would they say are ways of thinking that are being transformed?

They should then write their responses on an appropriate place on the mind chart.

Now, spend time asking the Holy Spirit to show each member of the group one or two ways He is challenging them to change – to think about more, or less, or to be transformed in how they think about them. Invite people to mark some arrows on their own chart to show this.

FINAL PRAYER

Invite the group members to place a hand on their thought audit activity sheets. If the sheet hasn't been used then maybe place a hand on their own head. Spend some time praying that, in view of God's mercy, our minds would be pleasing and holy. Pray for clear judgment and the revelation of God's gifts He has for us.

WORKSHEET: WHAT IS ON YOUR MIND?

Take some time to carry out a **thought audit** of your mind. It may be easiest to do this by casting your mind back over the past twenty-four hours, or the past week, month or year. What is on your mind a lot? What thoughts only pop up occasionally? Which of these ways of thinking seem to be **conformed to the pattern of this world** and which would you say are **being transformed?**

Write them on an appropriate place on the mind chart.

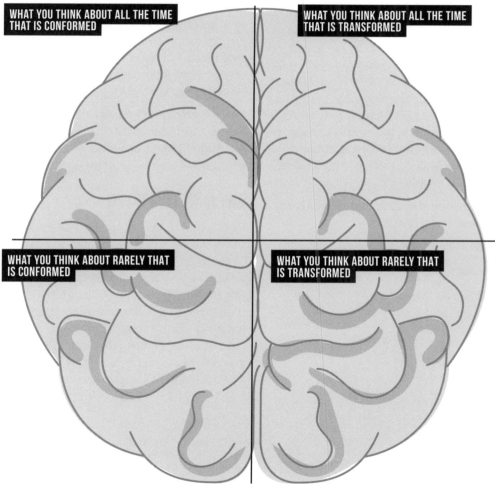

WHAT YOU THINK ABOUT ALL THE TIME THAT IS CONFORMED

WHAT YOU THINK ABOUT ALL THE TIME THAT IS TRANSFORMED

WHAT YOU THINK ABOUT RARELY THAT IS CONFORMED

WHAT YOU THINK ABOUT RARELY THAT IS TRANSFORMED

Now, ask the Holy Spirit to show you one or two ways of thinking He is challenging you to change – to think about more, or less, or to be transformed in how you think about them. Mark some arrows on the chart to show this.

TAKE HOME [1] DAILY RETREAT

Each day we need to stop and remind ourselves what is important. We can get so focused on the now that we forget to focus on the eternal. A daily six-minute retreat will help build the relationship with God that will sustain us today and tomorrow.

THREE MINUTES: BIBLE

Take out your Bible – either paper or digital.

We suggest you read brief passages, bit by bit, and allow yourself to take it in. If this is your first time reading the Bible, we recommend starting with a Gospel and then the book of Acts. You could use a study guide to provide passages to read if you wish or check out an annual Bible (for example, The Bible in One Year – NIV).

Take a short passage, read it, and ask yourself three questions.

1. What does this tell me about me?

2. What does this tell me about God?

3. What do I need to do to take the passage and live it?

TWO MINUTES: PRAY

God loves your voice. He loves to hear what you have to say. He loves to hear you cry, laugh and complain. Your prayers do not need to be clever. Simply say either in your mind or out loud what is happening in your life.

Share thanksgiving as well as your needs. Simply start by saying something like, hello God, Dear Father or God come and find me. Then just go for it.

ONE MINUTE: LISTEN

God wants to talk to you as well as listen. Take a moment to listen to Him. Sometimes you might get a sense of what he is saying. Some people talk about a feeling; you might just feel His presence. This is all positive and part of knowing God. If you hear nothing, don't get stressed. Sit still with God. When you are ready, end by saying Amen (means 'so be it').

[8]
SESSION 2:
A HEART OF FLESH

BIG IDEA

We have to allow what we believe to affect how we belong, what we love, and what we appreciate. Our hearts should be aligned with the heart of God. We want to have hearts that are broken for the things that break His. We can be openhearted or closed-hearted. We talk about people being broken-hearted and hard-hearted. It's the content of our hearts that shapes our characters, desires, and wishes. Our hearts lead us when it comes to prayer and relationship with God.

[Q] How is your heart? Take a moment and think about it. Is it broken, lonely, hard, compassionate, desperate, apathetic? This is just a suggestion; you will have your own words.

[Q] If someone was writing a paragraph on your tombstone about what you were passionate about and what you loved, what do you think they would write? Would God get a mention?

BUSYNESS, HURRY, AND OVERLOAD

Busyness is a problem in the modern world. In the 1960s we were told that technology would make us more productive and we would only be working one-third of the hours we once worked. The reality is, the opposite has happened. We have become busier and more stressed and anxious. We are more connected and more disconnected at the same time. This way of life has affected the lives of disciples. Michael Zigarelli in Freedom from Busyness makes this observation:

It may be the case that

1. *Christians are assimilating a culture of busyness, hurry and overload, which leads to...*

2. *God becoming more marginalised in Christians' lives, which leads to...*

3. *A deteriorating relationship with God, which leads to...*

4. *Christians becoming even more vulnerable to adopting secular assumptions about how to live, which leads to...*

5. *More conformity to culture of busyness, hurry and overload. And then the cycle begins again.*

Jesus reveals a different way of life. In the Gospels Jesus is always finding time to encounter strangers and sit with people who are on the edge. When we talk about following Jesus, I wonder if the major problem isn't following but walking off, leaving Jesus behind. Jesus might not have been seen as productive in the traditional way in His ministry. He was always going off to pray and spend time alone or with His Father. It's in a place of prayer that we slow our lives down to encounter God and allow our hearts to become aligned with God's.

PRAYER

Before reading the passage take a moment to pray. Invite the Holy Spirit to speak to the group through the passage. This is key each week. Praying before reading the Bible opens us up to God speaking and shows that we want to learn from Him as well as each other.

"'For I will take you out of the nations; I will gather you from all the countries and bring you back into your own land. I will sprinkle clean water on you, and you will be clean; I will cleanse you from all your impurities and from all your idols. I will give you a new heart and put a new spirit in you; I will remove from you your heart of stone and give you a heart of flesh. And I will put my Spirit in you and move you to follow my decrees and be careful to keep my laws. Then you will live in the land I gave your ancestors; you will be my people, and I will be your God. I will save you from all your uncleanness. I will call for the grain and make it plentiful and will not bring famine upon you. I will increase the fruit of the trees and the crops of the field, so that you will no longer suffer disgrace among the nations because of famine. Then you will remember your evil ways and wicked deeds, and you will loathe yourselves for your sins and detestable practices. I want you to know that I am not doing this for your sake, declares the Sovereign Lord. Be ashamed and disgraced for your conduct, people of Israel!'"

[R] EZEKIEL 36:24–32

Having read the passage, pause for a moment or two. Some groups may like to read the passage twice – maybe with two different voices or from different translations.

Start by facilitating an open discussion on people's reactions to the passage, using questions like:

[Q] What jumps out of the passage for you?

[Q] Is there anything you struggle with/don't understand?

[Q] Are there any new connections you can make within or beyond this passage?

ACTIVITY

WORKSHEET – PART 1

Using the worksheet have the group spend 10 minutes reflecting on what a heart of stone and a heart of flesh look like in practice. They can use words like cold, disconnected, unhappy, warm, energized, loving.

[Q] The passage tells us that God wants His Spirit to be poured into our hearts to see our hearts renewed. The same Spirit that raised Christ from the grave is the Spirit God wants to place in and around our hearts. He does this so that our hearts might guide us to live like He intends. How do you think our hearts might be different after this has happened?

[Q] "I will cleanse you from all your impurities and from all your idols." Idols misdirect our hearts to look at the wrong things and take our attention away from God-things. How have you seen this at work in your life?

[Q] The passage talks about clean and unclean hearts. To what extent are areas of sin and brokenness in your life being changed by Jesus?

[Q] In what areas do you sense God challenging you at this time?

CLUES YOUR HEART MAY BE HARD OR HARDENING

1. You don't feel like talking to anyone.

One clear way that you can easily see if your heart is hard is if you find yourself shutting down sensitive topics. In this situation you might struggle to have any conversation with substance. It's very normal for us to have areas of our lives that we aren't comfortable facing in public. We must be aware that there is a danger of becoming someone who avoids vulnerability for defence reasons.

2. You might be low on patience or have no interest in other people.

If you have been giving out and supporting lots of people without boundaries you can become low on patience and detach yourself from others, showing no interest in them or their lives. You may also struggle to hear them talking again about something you have lost interest in. It may be a sign of compassion fatigue where we have simply become overwhelmed with others' lives so we have closed down our emotions towards others.

3. Other people's advice seems bad to you and they are always wrong in your mind.

Remember the story of Pharaoh, who, having hardened his heart, refused to listen to the pleas of Moses to allow justice to happen. In situations like this multiple people may be suggesting something to you that you find good reason to disprove or disagree with. You have become closed to others' wisdom. This may stem from pride or arrogance.

4. You're unable to love anyone or find forgiveness for someone.

Having had a situation blow up in your face or a person significantly hurt you, it is possible for your heart to reject love in the future and reject forgiveness as a way of holding power in the relationship. If we don't forgive other people we can stop ourselves and them from moving on, and even justify anger as right. The impact this can have is for future relationships to be jeopardized and distrust for others grows. In the long term, our relationship with God also suffers as we struggle to feel loved and forgiven.

5. You can't be happy for someone else's success, only your own.

When our hearts are hard we try to hold power, be powerful, and reject others' power. If someone has a good news story or happy moment and we are not allowing ourselves or them to enjoy it, then there is a good chance we are holding onto hurt as a way of having power over a situation. Envy will always cause us to hate someone else and the good they have. The outworking of this is that we spend time hoping they will always fail.

6. You don't feel anything about the things that you should.

You do not feel shameful of your actions; you justify them, telling yourself it's your right to feel like this. You also don't feel guilty when you know you have done something you shouldn't because you have found a way to justify it. Hardening our hearts can mean we justify things that simply should not be justified. We become people who lose sight of what the key indicators are in our lives for sin. We become insensitive to feelings of shame and guilt. Once we are in this place we will justify anything for our own desires.

WORKSHEET – PART 2

Return to the activity sheet. Ask the group to wait on the Holy Spirit and choose two issues on the "heart of stone" side, for God to transform their hearts, and two desires on the "heart of flesh" side that can be developed. Those phrases should be used to complete the following sentence:

God will remove my heart of _____

and give me a heart of _____

FINAL PRAYER

Pray using the sentences the group has just written on their sheets. Praying in pairs and praying sentences over each other is a successful exercise here. However, if the group is not confident praying like this they could pray these personally for themselves. Conclude by praying together that God would soften hearts, that hearts would be flesh, and that they would beat in time with His.

WORKSHEET: HEARTS OF STONE AND FLESH

STEP 1

Think about words or phrases that may describe a heart of stone and a heart of flesh. Take some time to write on the "heart of stone" side of the diagram words that spring to mind that sum up this heart state. Do the same for the "heart of flesh". Try to be as specific and as broad reaching as you can.

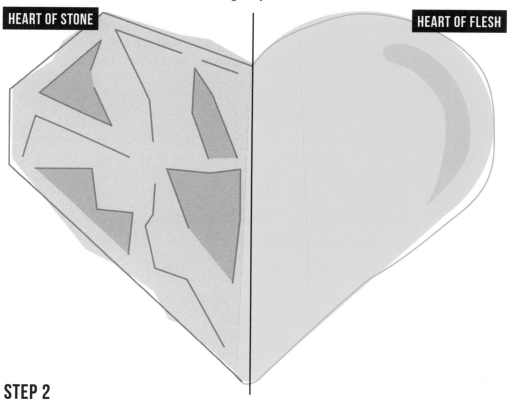

HEART OF STONE

HEART OF FLESH

STEP 2

Ask the Holy Spirit to draw attention to any words on the left that describe your heart and any on the right that you long for more of in your heart. Circle them and use them to complete the sentences below. (For example: God will remove my heart of *selfishness* and give me a heart of *compassion*.)

God will remove my heart of _____

and give me a heart of _____

God will remove my heart of _____

and give me a heart of _____

TAKE HOME [2]
HOW TO READ THE BIBLE

We need God to speak to us, both in our minds and our hearts. If we are left to our own devices the world and culture around us will shape us, not God. Here we spend some time letting God shape us using an old Bible reading method called the 'Swedish Bible Study Method'. This shaping of your minds can happen when we engage with the Holy Spirit through the Bible. Start by taking the Gospel of Matthew (or another gospel). As you read or listen to a short section of the Bible, take a moment to pray that God will be speaking to you through it, then use these questions to help you hear Him.

WHAT JUMPS OUT TO ME?

This should be something in the passage that grabs your attention, maybe challenge, inspiration or something weird.

ANY BURNING QUESTIONS?

This is anything you find hard to understand, or wish you could ask the writer. No question is too silly.

WHAT ABOUT GOD?

God is not made up of our imagination but made us to be friends with Him. What does this show about His nature and intentions?

WHAT ABOUT PEOPLE?

We were made in His image but have been distorted by ego, fear and pain. What does this show of who we were made to be?

WHAT AM I GOING TO DO?

We are invited by Jesus to live life to the full and we learn by doing. What are you going to do about what you've read?

[9]
SESSION 3:
YOUR HANDS ARE NOT YOUR OWN

BIG IDEA

We can gain knowledge and information about Jesus and believe this is discipleship. Discipleship is more than just believing what the teacher says, studying theology, arguing with the best agnostics, reading weighty Christian books, etc. Discipleship is *following* and *copying*. We will never get our hands to do anything if our hearts do not belong to Jesus. Making the connection between what our head knows and what our heart longs for is key to getting our hands serving Jesus. In this session, we will look at what was in Moses' hands (very little), but when God blessed what was in Moses' hands and his heart was willing, God's people were set free from oppression.

[Q] What stops you from having a faith that is active in serving others?

[Q] Ask the group to look down at their hands. Ask them in the last twenty-four hours, or the last week, how much time their hands have been used for God's work?

Both questions can sound judgmental but they are simply meant to raise questions for us. We can all improve how we use what we have for Jesus.

DID YOU KNOW?

The word "Christian" only appears in the Bible three times but the name "disciple" appears 263 times. This should indicate to us that Jesus is looking for people who not only believe the gospel but also live it out day to day. James 2:14–17 challenges us to live lives of faith that have flesh and blood put onto our beliefs.

[ʺ]

What good is it, my brothers and sisters, if someone claims to have faith but has no deeds? Can such faith save them? Suppose a brother or a sister is without clothes and daily food. If one of you says to them, "Go in peace; keep warm and well fed," but does nothing about their physical needs, what good is it? In the same way, faith by itself, if it is not accompanied by action, is dead.

Faith and deeds: this is what Jesus is looking for in us, a life of faith lived out.

PRAYER

Before reading the passage take a moment to pray. Invite the Holy Spirit to speak to the group through the passage. This is key each week. Praying before reading the Bible opens us up to God speaking and shows that we want to learn from Him as well as each other.

Moses answered, "What if they do not believe me or listen to me and say, 'The Lord did not appear to you'?"

Then the Lord said to him, "What is that in your hand?"

"A staff," he replied.

The Lord said, "Throw it on the ground."

Moses threw it on the ground and it became a snake, and he ran from it. Then the Lord said to him, "Reach out your hand and take it by the tail." So Moses reached out and took hold of the snake and it turned back into a staff in his hand. "This," said the Lord, "is so that they may believe that the Lord, the God of their fathers – the God of Abraham, the God of Isaac and the God of Jacob – has appeared to you."

[R] EXODUS 4:1–5

Having read the passage, pause for a moment or two. Some groups may like to read the passage twice – maybe with two different voices or from different translations.

Start by facilitating an open discussion on people's reactions to the passage, using questions like:

[Q] What jumps out of the passage for you?

[Q] Is there anything you struggle with/don't understand?

[Q] Are there any new connections you can make within or beyond this passage?

[Q] "Then the Lord said to him, 'What is that in your hand?'" God says the same to us. What do you have in your hands? What has God blessed you with? Don't revert to the default Christian humble answer of "little". What gifts or experiences has God given you?

ACTIVITY

WORKSHEET – PART 1

Ask the group to take time on the worksheet to draw out the gifts, talents, and training they have in their hands. Participants may feel that they use or are confident using certain gifts – write these in the palm of the hand. Some participants may feel unsure of their gifts or feel they don't have many opportunities to use them– write these around the fingertips. Encourage the group to be broad in their definition of gifts, talents, and training. Don't just go for what would be seen as spiritual gifts. Examples could be as wide ranging as painting, teaching, repairing objects, baking, or accountancy.

DIE TO OURSELVES

Mark 8:34 powerfully reminds us that as disciples we are to give everything we have over to Jesus. Jesus turns to his disciples and says, "Whoever wants to be my disciple must deny themselves and take up their cross and follow me." "Deny" themselves can also be translated as "die to" themselves. In other words, a disciple is someone who is dying to the idea of his or her own rights, time, status, ego, power, security, safety, space, money, and resources to trust in the will of Jesus. So what should discipleship be for us? It should be the lifelong adventure of submitting obediently our minds and thinking (heads), our passions and desires (hearts), and our daily activity, resources, and gifts (hands, and all in them) to the will and love of God.

[Q] What would you struggle to submit to Jesus? What would you want to cling on to?

WORKSHEET – PART 2

This worksheet can be downloaded double-sided from the website: wearemakingdisciples.com.

This will work well in a group that knows each other reasonably well. Get the group to turn their sheets over and put their names on them. Put all sheets in the middle and encourage the group to list the gifts they see in one another on their corresponding sheet.

Ask the group to individually reflect on what others see in them.

SUGGESTION: In a group that does not know one another well, encourage the group to find someone they know and trust to fill in the reverse.

[Q] It's only when Moses throws what he has before God that God then can do something with it. Have you ever offered God what you have in your hands – your gifts, talents, skills, and resources? The reality for some of us is that we have offered what we think is worthwhile and failed to offer what we think is useless. We can't determine what is unusable; that is our Father's role.

[Q] Moses became so committed to others that he risked his life for them. All of this was because he had an encounter with God. How committed are you to God's people? Does being committed to Christian believers (the church) demand enough of your time and energy?

[Q] God called Moses to use his gifts so that others would be set free from slavery and so that they, in turn, would use their gifts for Him. Have you thought about your role in helping others use their gifts? Are there others like you whom you could invest in and show what they have in their hands are treasures too?

God invested in Moses; Moses invested in Joshua. Can you think about three people whom you could invest in?

NAMES:

[1] _____

[2] _____

[3] _____

FINAL PRAYER

Finish the session by giving God each person's gifts and creating space to pray for the names they have listed. If appropriate, you could take some oil and anoint one another's hands for His kingdom work.

WORKSHEET: WHAT IS IN YOUR HANDS? [1]

STEP 1

Take time to reflect on the gifts and talents you feel you may have. Write them on the hand – use the palm to show those you use regularly and the finger tips to write those in which you feel less confident or have less opportunity to grow.

GIFTS AND TALENTS I DON'T USE OFTEN/FEEL CONFIDENT IN:

GIFTS AND TALENTS I USE REGULARLY/FEEL CONFIDENT IN:

WORKSHEET: WHAT IS IN YOUR HANDS? [2]

STEP 2

Having reflected on your own gifts and talents, write your name on this side of the sheet and give others in the group a chance to write the gifts and talents that they see in you.

NAME: _____

WE SEE THESE GIFTS AND TALENTS IN YOU:

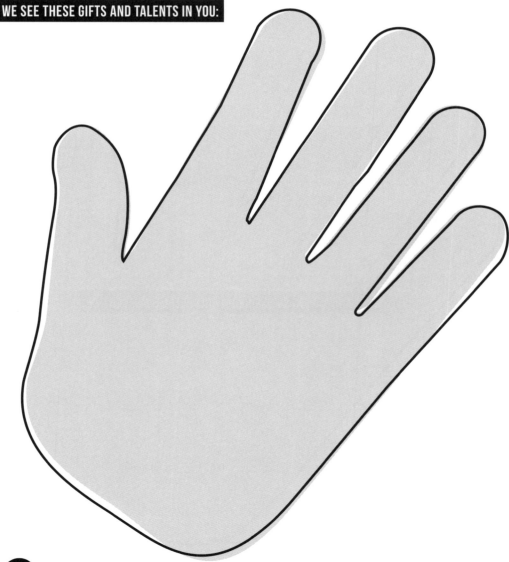

TAKE HOME [3]: PRACTISE GENEROCITY

God has generously given each of us so much. When we think about giving what we have in our hands, we must think about our time, energy, gifts and all of our many resources. It has often been said the wallet is the last thing to be entrusted to God. Traditionally giving money has been called tithing. Tithing was the practice of giving 10% of our income to God as a sign of our love, worship and trust.

PRACTICE GIVING THIS WEEK.

1. If you have not already, set up regular giving to your church community. When we use the resources we have to worship God we become invested in His work and wish to partner further with Him.

2. Look at your time as something in your hands. Could you take an evening a week to do something that would serve others. This may involve clearing time in your busy week. Serving God should not be the leftover time we have once we have done everything we want; placing God in our spare time makes Him a hobby. Actively look for some charity work or ministry you can give a few hours to each week and sign up.

[10]
SESSION 4: LEARNING AND REMEMBERING TOGETHER

BIG IDEA

God has created us for community, to learn and grow together. This would be an excellent time to reflect on the communities we are part of, our commitment to them, and how we both learn and help others learn in these contexts. An obvious place to start would be local church and small group membership but there may be other communities people want to discuss as well, such as the workplace, the local community, or even the extended family.

[Q] Can you think of a time you changed your opinion on something? Who or what circumstances led to this change?

[Q] What are the communities you are part of and how do they help you to learn more about God, life, and faith?

CHURCH IS HARD BUT WHAT WE NEED

Being married is hard work; it challenges us and exposes our vulnerabilities. In marriage we are forced to realise how self-centred we are, how broken we are, and how shallow we are. For those of us not married we will be able to recognize how a deep commitment to another human will bring out our own insecurities. The same is true of the church. It's hard to be part of the church because it forces us to realize that we are egotistical, prideful, and self-centred. The church is a hard place for many of us but it is also the antidote that Jesus has given all of us. Jesus calls the church to *be* together rather than to *go to* church. The reality is people criticize the church from afar, saying, "I'd never be a part of that", or keep leaving churches looking for the mythical perfect community. Yet the best place for us to be is in this family and for us to work at creating a true Jesus community by allowing it to shape and transform us. The church is a gathering of people all pledging allegiance to something bigger. It's a new kind of community where broken and damaged people gather together with the purpose of becoming an army of light.

PRAYER

Before reading the passage take a moment to pray. Invite the Holy Spirit to speak to the group through the passage. This is key each week. Praying before reading the Bible opens us up to God speaking and shows that we want to learn from Him as well as each other.

These are the commands, decrees and laws the Lord your God directed me to teach you to observe in the land that you are crossing the Jordan to possess, so that you, your children and their children after them may fear the Lord your God as long as you live by keeping all his decrees and commands that I give you, and so that you may enjoy long life. Hear, Israel, and be careful to obey so that it may go well with you and that you may increase greatly in a land flowing with milk and honey, just as the Lord, the God of your ancestors, promised you.

Hear, O Israel: The Lord our God, the Lord is one. Love the Lord your God with all your heart and with all your soul and with all your strength. These commandments that I give you today are to be on your hearts. Impress them on your children. Talk about them when you sit at home and when you walk along the road, when you lie down and when you get up. Tie them as symbols on your hands and bind them on your foreheads. Write them on the doorframes of your houses and on your gates.

[R] DEUTERONOMY 6:1–9

Having read the passage, pause for a moment or two. Some groups may like to read the passage twice – maybe with two different voices and from different translations.

Start by facilitating an open discussion on people's reactions to the passage, using questions like:

[Q] What jumps out of the passage for you?

[Q] Is there anything you struggle with/don't understand?

[Q] Are there any new connections you can make within or beyond this passage?

[Q] The Israelites were called to learn and remember together in order to "fear the Lord your God" and "obey". How do you respond to words like this? What might it mean for us today?

[Q] How well do you respond to God's teachings that are in place to instruct and direct us?

Are you someone who is un-teachable?

Someone who doesn't like it but gets on with it?

Someone who welcomes Gods teaching?

[Q] If "commandments" means "God's way of life for us", how can we be sure that this is central to the membership of our community?

[Q] How can we be sure that as we learn together this impacts our hands and hearts and how we live beyond church?

[Q] "Love the Lord your God with all your heart and with all your soul and with all your strength." This line is about giving everything to God, loving God with everything we have. Is this something you welcome or find easy? Is it something you struggle with or reject?

ACTIVITY

WORKSHEET

Hand out copies of the Venn-diagram worksheet (on page 46) so the participants can review their Discipleship Shapes. Prayerfully reflecting on the last few weeks, ask the group to pick a question from the wheel for each area in which they are seeing, or want to see, more progress.

Having done this, reflect on how connected their heads, hands and hearts are in loving God. Is the way they think about God (head) in or out of sync with the way they relate to God (heart)? Write a percentage in each overlap and highlight an area where God wants more connection.

[Q] Deuteronomy 6:7 reads "Impress them on your children. Talk about them when you sit at home and when you walk along the road, when you lie down and when you get up." The impression you get here is that we should be talking about God and reflecting upon His ways all the time. We should be wrestling with God and our lives; we should be teaching each other and working with each other. How much of your faith do you discuss with others?

[Q] How do we build a community where questions are welcomed and encouraged and help us to grow together?

FINAL QUESTION

[Q] What can you do this week to ensure your interactions with others lead to deeper and richer learning both for you and them?

FINAL PRAYER

What follows is a suggested prayer to use with the group. Feel free to create or use your own. End the session by giving the group time to pray and respond.

Holy risk-taker, wonderful God,

You create us out of Your deep, exuberant love

And in great hope.

More than that, You make us in Your own image;

We are humbled and enlivened by Your faith in us.

You call us to love You with all that we have, but as we struggle to do so help us to move forwards, giving more of ourselves to Your hand.

May our minds be transformed.

May our hearts be soft, merciful, and wanting.

May our hands be ready to serve, to act, and to give.

(A moment of silence)

Forgive us where we have been arrogant with our beliefs.

Forgive us when our hearts have been hardened to Your teaching.

Forgive us when our hands have remained in our pockets clinging to what we have.

Release us from all that harms us; help us to turn again, and again, from selfishness to selflessness – so that we grow in wisdom and maturity towards the day when we become perfect bearers of Your image.

Amen

WORKSHEET: HEAD, HEART, AND HANDS

LOVING GOD WITH OUR HEAD [MIND], HEART [SOUL], AND HANDS [STRENGTH].

This sheet reflects progress in the course so far. Using the Discipleship Shape, draw out a question from each section (head, hands, heart) that you have either grown in over the last few weeks or that you feel God has highlighted as a potential growth area. Write each one in the appropriate circle.

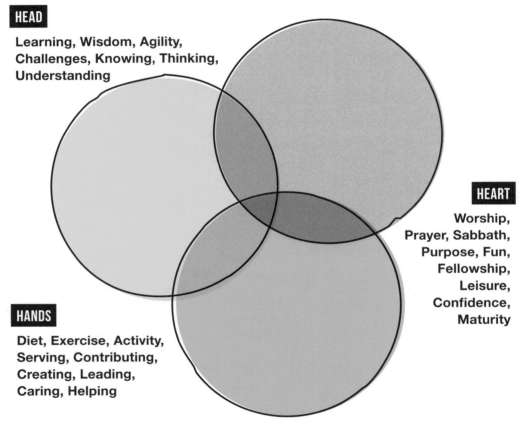

HEAD

Learning, Wisdom, Agility, Challenges, Knowing, Thinking, Understanding

HEART

Worship, Prayer, Sabbath, Purpose, Fun, Fellowship, Leisure, Confidence, Maturity

HANDS

Diet, Exercise, Activity, Serving, Contributing, Creating, Leading, Caring, Helping

God calls us to be connected beings – how connected are your head, hands, and heart? In each overlap write a percentage to show how connected you feel these areas are in your life. For example, if your heart and the way you act are completely in sync, put 100 percent. If the way you think about God and the way you relate to Him are completely disconnected, put 0 percent there. This is just subjective so don't be overly worried about the numbers.

Where is God calling you to be more connected?

TAKE HOME FOUR: PRAY

Getting off the ground with prayer can be hard for many new Christians; you just don't know where to start. We want to take the pressure off and let you enjoy prayer stress-free.

Prayer is the greatest and most powerful weapon we have as followers of Jesus. With prayer we communicate with the Father who loves us. Remember, nothing is impossible with him. Getting yourself into a daily rhythm of praying should become as easy as breathing.

Here are some suggestions to help you as you begin praying.

WHO AND WHAT TO PRAY FOR?

- Your family and friends
- Your neighbourhood
- Nation and its leaders
- Those you want to come to faith
- Those in need and other Christians worldwide.
- Those you find challenging
- Your church family
- Your workplace, the place you spend most of your time.

WAYS TO PRAY

Praying doesn't have to be done on your knees at the end of your bed with eyes closed. Prayer is something active and dynamic. Try praying while walking. Maybe writing your prayers down in a journal works best for you. Write them on post-it notes and stick them on your wall. Perhaps doodling while you pray or even doodle as a prayer.

Draw what you want to see happen. Set an alarm to go off at points in the day to remind you to pray.

If you find prayer a struggle, simply use the Lords Prayer. The Lord's Prayer was never meant to be a religious mumble prayer, but a passionate war cry calling in God's kingdom.

> *Our Father in heaven,*
> *hallowed be Your name,*
> *Your kingdom come,*
> *Your will be done,*
> *on earth as in heaven.*
> *Give us today our daily bread.*
> *Forgive us our sins, as we forgive those who sin against us.*
> *Lead us not into temptation, but deliver us from evil.*
> *For the kingdom, the power, and the glory are Yours*
> *now and forever.*
> *Amen.*

[11]
SESSION 5:
IMPACTING OUR WORLD

If offering an additional week is an option or necessary, there is extra material prepared to further explore discipleship. Also included are materials to establish and practically begin a personal mission. Remember that you can return to your Discipleship Shape and spend time looking at what might have changed.

BIG IDEA

God wants the good He has done in our lives to be a reflection and a blessing to those around us, both in our communities and the world. To stop with our heads and hearts is to say that His work in our lives is only for us. But He has called us to love, to serve, and to point people to Him. The great commission makes it our mission to tell the world of Jesus' salvation and to make disciples. This is how discipleship replicates itself; when we draw near to Jesus we, in turn, can draw others to Him.

Jesus didn't just die to save you *from* something – sin – but *for* something – mission.

[Q] What does "mission" mean to you?

[Q] In what ways do you find it hard to share what you know and believe about God with others?

PRAYER

Before reading the following passages take a moment to pray. Invite the Holy Spirit to speak to the group through the passage. This is key each week. Praying before reading the Bible opens us up to God speaking and shows that we want to learn from Him as well as each other.

The mission of all humanity:

> *Now the Lord God had planted a garden in the east, in Eden; and there he put the man he had formed. The Lord God made all kinds of trees grow out of the ground – trees that were pleasing to the eye and good for food. In the middle of the garden were the tree of life and the tree of the knowledge of good and evil.*

A river watering the garden flowed from Eden; from there it was separated into four headwaters. The name of the first is the Pishon; it winds through the entire land of Havilah, where there is gold. (The gold of that land is good; aromatic resin and onyx are also there.) The name of the second river is the Gihon; it winds through the entire land of Cush. The name of the third river is the Tigris; it runs along the east side of Ashur. And the fourth river is the Euphrates.

The Lord God took the man and put him in the Garden of Eden to work it and take care of it. And the Lord God commanded the man, "You are free to eat from any tree in the garden..."

[R] GENESIS 2:8–16

The mission Jesus gave His followers:

Then the eleven disciples went to Galilee, to the mountain where Jesus had told them to go. When they saw him, they worshipped him; but some doubted. Then Jesus came to them and said, "All authority in heaven and on earth has been given to me. Therefore go and make disciples of all nations, baptizing them in the name of the Father and of the Son and of the Holy Spirit, and teaching them to obey everything I have commanded you. And surely I am with you always, to the very end of the age."

[R] MATTHEW 28:16–20

Having read the passages, pause for a moment or two. Some groups may like to read the passages twice – maybe with two different voices or different translations.

Start by facilitating an open discussion on people's reactions to the passage, using questions like:

What jumps out of the passages for you?

Is there anything you struggle with/don't understand?

Are there any new connections you can make within or beyond these passages?

DRESSING AND BLESSING

The mission of God is to save people as well as creation. In the Genesis 2 passage we are told that humanity is placed in the garden to work and care for creation.

The word "work" is the Hebrew word *ovd*, which can also be translated as to serve and to dress, in the sense of making presentable, like a servant would serve and dress his master. The word "care" is the Hebrew word *shomr*, which can be translated as keep, preserve, protect, watch, bring justice to or speak out for, in a similar way to that of a prophet.

A good analogy for what God is communicating here is that of a baby. The baby can't feed itself or wash itself, and neither can it dress itself; the baby needs 24/7 care with someone looking over it constantly. The baby can't protect itself or stand up for itself and, on occasion, may need someone to speak out and bring justice for it, as it has no voice of its own.

[Q] God placed people in the garden to "rule" or "subdue" creation. Some translations say dress, protect or care for. Why would God care for the planet? Surely He cares more about people?

The answer is an obvious no. God cares for people and the home He created for them. God's mission is for us to reconnect people with God and people with creation.

[Q] Both commissions in Genesis and Matthew are about authority. Jesus gives us authority over creation and authority to lead people to faith. Which of these two commissions has been your primary commission? Why?

[Q] Are there any connections between these two commissions from Genesis and Matthew? Can we do one without the other?

[Q] Both of these commissions give us our purpose. Our purpose is to live a life that is Christ-like, creating, recreating, and reconnecting with others. Have you ever thought about this?

[Q] Both of these passages are about activity and engaging. Where has your faith not done this in the past? Could this be something to change?

ACTIVITY

WORKSHEET

Using the "Spirals" worksheet (on page 51), spend some time reflecting upon your mission activity in the religious spheres through to the non-religious. For the purpose of this activity we are thinking about mission in terms of evangelism and Christian influence.

FINAL PRAYER

Spend some time praying for your personal and church mission. Who are the people you are investing in and trying to reveal to Jesus? Spend time as a group praying over those you are wanting to see move towards Jesus. Pray for encounters that help you play your part in their conversion.

WORKSHEET: SPIRALS

Jesus tells the disciples to take the gospel from Jerusalem (religious headquarters) to Judea (kind of religious), to Samaria (other religions), to the ends of the earth (non-religious).

This spiral out is the call of all disciples to go from the religious to the wider world. On the spiral track your weekly influence. Name people and places you interact with that, as a disciple, are part of your mission.

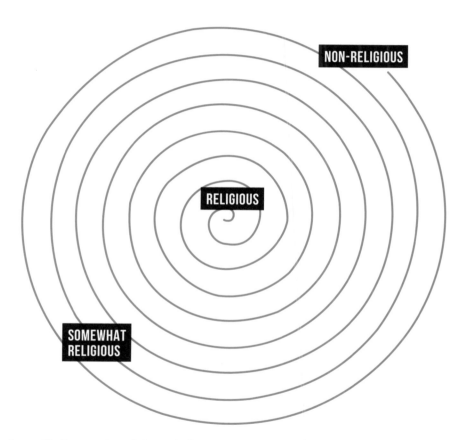

Starting with the centre of the spiral, write the name of the Christian community you live in, or the group of Christian friends you would call your church. As you journey out from the centre mark the growing non-religious places in which you travel. On the last third of the spiral think about the places you would fear going – places where you would struggle to travel because it would take you out of your comfort zone.

[Q] Who are the people, places or streets that you would struggle to visit?

[Q] Who is your Samaria and the ends of the earth?

TAKE HOME [5]: PASS IT ON

Jesus told the disciples to pass on what they learned from Him. So they did pass it on, all the way to YOU. You have now learned about Jesus and started on your journey of faith. This means you have been entrusted with a great treasure to share with others. Telling people about Jesus should be as easy as telling people about a new product you have bought or a meal you have eaten or a baby being born. Telling people about your new faith should be joyful and exciting.

There is one lie the evil one wants to convince you of. He will tell you that you're not ready to share your faith because you don't know enough. This is simply not true. You don't need to know enough if you know Jesus because he is enough. Be confident that what you have to share is brilliant and needs to be given away.

HERE ARE FIVE THINGS TO REMEMBER WHEN SHARING THIS GOOD NEWS.

1. Your life is a great story to share. Simply telling people your story, sharing what it means to you to find faith in Jesus is inspirational. Perhaps you could explain how it wasn't what you expected. Your story is full of exciting, fantastic stuff. Many people simply haven't given it any thought. People who know you will see the change your faith is making to you and by walking them through your journey to faith, you are offering the best witness to them.

2. We earn the right to be heard by listening to others. Don't expect to be listened to if you don't listen to others. Become a good listener. The Bible says that Jesus became a friend of sinners, so you do the same. Become a good friend by offering a safe place for others to share their concerns, worries, stresses and whatever else life might be throwing at them. There is no need for you to commentate their thoughts or actions. Just be with them.

3. People are looking for a cure. We are all broken and Jesus comes to heal our brokenness. When we are sick, we go to the doctor and relay our symptoms because that's what you see. The doctor sees the actual problem and can give a prognosis and a cure. We see loneliness, suffering, distrust, stress and we become overwhelmed by them. But we also know the ultimate cure, Jesus. Jesus came to die not for our symptoms but for our sins which are causing the symptoms. Our friends wake up with symptoms that leave them in pain so as people who are attempting to help, we need to start with their symptoms. We show them the disease (sin), and take them to the ultimate cure (Jesus).

4. Keep it simple and clear. We don't need to complicate things. Simply tell people the good news that Jesus loves them and wants them to be free from the symptoms of their sin as well as the sin itself. John 3:16 says, "For God so loved the world that he gave his one and only Son, that whoever believes in him shall not perish but have eternal life" (NIV).

5. Pray. Always pray for those you want to see come to faith. Prayer leading up to sharing your faith with them invites God into the movement and the relationship.

NOTES

_____

_____

_____

_____

_____

_____

_____

_____

_____

_____

_____

_____

_____

_____

_____

_____

[12]
SESSION 6:
BEING PEOPLE WHO DO
WHAT WE BELIEVE

BIG IDEA

We have seen how important it is to commit our heads and hearts to God but those two commitments must lead to our hands being ready to both praise and serve Jesus.

It can be easy to read the Bible and become knowledgeable of different scriptures, but it must not be only to recite passages and argue theological points. The gospel can be clearly articulated like this: "We are saved by grace through faith in Jesus." Our faith is then demonstrated not just by what we *say*, but by what we *do*. It's in the activity of our faith lived out that people see Jesus in us. Our hands need to be committed to Jesus so that we not only read the gospel but also live it.

[Q] Are there any Bible passages you've read in the past couple of weeks that have challenged you in your daily living?

[Q] What distractions stop you from fully engaging in serving others, or worshipping God in action?

RULE OF LIFE FOR THE CHRISTIANS

You might like to reference this quote from Aristides, a Greek Roman historian from AD 137. In his time, the church had become known for being people who lived like Jesus. Our desire is to be people who live our lives in such a way the world sees the works of Jesus through the church.

["]

Oh emperor, it is the Christians that have sought and found the truth, for they acknowledge God. They do not keep for themselves the goods entrusted to them. They do not covet what belongs to others, but they show love to their neighbours. They do not do to another what they would not like done to themselves. They speak gently to those who oppress them, and in this way, they make their enemies their friends. It has become their passion to do good to their enemies. They live in the awareness of their own smallness. Every one of them who has anything gives ungrudgingly to the one who has nothing. And if any of them sees a

PRAYER

Before reading the passage take a moment to pray. Invite the Holy Spirit to speak to the group through the passage. This is key each week. Praying before reading the Bible opens us up to God speaking and shows that we want to learn from Him as well as each other.

So I say, walk by the Spirit, and you will not gratify the desires of the flesh. For the flesh desires what is contrary to the Spirit, and the Spirit what is contrary to the flesh. They are in conflict with each other, so that you are not to do whatever you want. But if you are led by the Spirit, you are not under the law.

The acts of the flesh are obvious: sexual immorality, impurity and debauchery; idolatry and witchcraft; hatred, discord, jealousy, fits of rage, selfish ambition, dissensions, factions and envy; drunkenness, orgies, and the like. I warn you, as I did before, that those who live like this will not inherit the kingdom of God.

But the fruit of the Spirit is love, joy, peace, forbearance, kindness, goodness, faithfulness, gentleness and self-control. Against such things there is no law. Those who belong to Christ Jesus have crucified the flesh with its passions and desires. Since we live by the Spirit, let us keep in step with the Spirit. Let us not become conceited, provoking and envying each other.

[R] GALATIANS 5:16–26

Having read the passage, pause for a moment or two. Some groups may like to read the passage twice – maybe with two different voices or different translations.

Start by facilitating an open discussion on people's reactions to the passage, using questions like:

[Q] What jumps out of the passage for you?

[Q] Is there anything you struggle with/don't understand?

[Q] Are there any new connections you can make within or beyond this passage?

[Q] The passage lists so much that a disciple should turn away from and reject. Did anything on the list particularly jump out at you as we read the passage? Are there any you find yourself particularly susceptible to?

[Q] The passage suggests that the Spirit wants to produce fruit in our lives. Write down the fruits in list form: love, joy, peace, forbearance, kindness, goodness, faithfulness, gentleness, and self-control. Are there people you know that particularly excel in any of these fruits? What impact does that have on those around them?

[Q] Which fruits of the Spirit appeal to you personally? Are there any you struggle with or simply wish to grow/develop?

[Q] We all have unique testimonies and journeys of faith. After reading the passage, are there specific areas in your life that have dramatically changed since submitting your hands to Jesus? Can you explain how this transformation came about?

[Q] What are the keys to transformation that this passage offers? How do these run counter to the philosophy of "just try harder" we are often offered in church?

ACTIVITY

WORKSHEET

Ephesians 4 talks of the fruits in our lives, both positive and negative, that flow from a life led by the Spirit or the flesh.

Have the group list negative fruits they would like to get rid of and those from Ephesians 4 they would like to grow in on the worksheet on page 58. Ask them to allow the Holy Spirit to speak to their hearts and reveal what work He might need to do within to make them, for example, more loving or less full of rage. Write some of these on the roots.

[Q] How would you use a passage like this to discuss your faith with a friend who isn't a Christian?

REFLECTION POINT

At this point in the course, we would encourage the participants to review the Discipleship Shape. Has anything changed since starting the course? Would anything have moved towards the centre? Take a few moments to reflect upon what might have changed for you.

FINAL PRAYER

We want to be disciples who reject old ways of behaving for new Jesus-centred behaviours. End this session by confessing sin and accepting new life in Him.

Lord, we ask for Your forgiveness
For all the ways we have wounded others this week,
For our careless thoughts,
For our thoughtless deeds,
For times we have not loved but caused distress.

Breathe Your life once more into our tired and weary lives, that the wounds may heal.
Though our sins may be as scarlet, may they be white as snow.
May we know the transforming gift of Your mercy and grace now and forever.

Now place on us our new selves. Would we be people who are marked by kindness, compassionate and loving to all. Would we be people who are quick to forgive and quick to act. Would we be people who do what we believe should be done.

We say yes to You Jesus and Your ways.

Amen

WORKSHEET: FRUITS AND ROOTS

Which of the marks of the "life of the flesh" from this passage do you feel challenged to deal with in your own life? Write these on the fruits on the left of the diagram.

Which of the fruits of the "life of the Spirit" from this passage do you feel particularly challenged to develop? Write these on the fruits on the right of the diagram.

Fruits come from being led by the Spirit or by our own flesh. Prayerfully invite the Holy Spirit to show you the work He wants to do in your life to help you deal with and grow in these areas. For example, what does He need to do in your heart to help you be more loving or less prone to fits of rage? Write your thoughts on the roots.

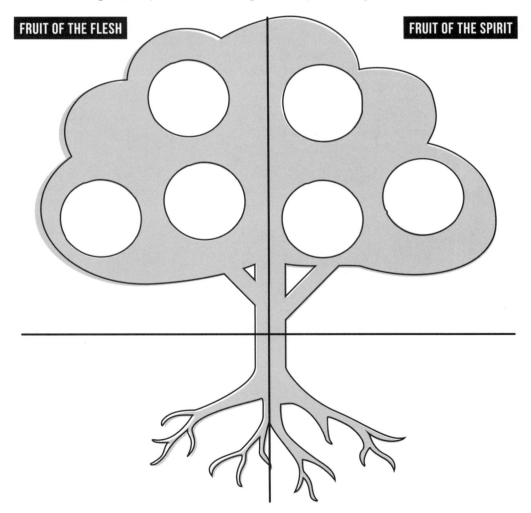

FRUIT OF THE FLESH

FRUIT OF THE SPIRIT

TAKE HOME [6]: PRACTISE THE FRUITS

We all have two natures, that of good and that of self-serving. It has been said in the past that we have two dogs. The dog of 'self' who loves ego and pride and the dog of goodness who loves the way of Jesus. We have to choose which dog we will feed each day. Starve the one and feed the other. Choosing to walk in the fruits of the Spirit is about choosing to feed the dog of faith and hope.

Each day this week look and explore a way of living out one of these fruits as a practice of growing in the Spirit. Some days will be harder than others. You may want to generate your own idea or take the suggestion below.

DAY 1: LOVE

Send someone a text telling them how much you appreciate them today.

DAY 2: JOY

Choose to be thankful for the small things. "Thank you for driving the train so I can get to work".

DAY 3: PEACE AND PATIENCE

On the hour take a moment to breathe and centre yourself. Invite God's Spirit to rest within you.

DAY 4: KINDNESS AND GENEROSITY

Do something today that is kind and will not be found out.

DAY 5: GOODNESS AND GENTLENESS

Take the opportunity to show love and respect to someone who is 'pushing your buttons' with even temper and strength under control.

DAY 6: FAITHFULNESS

Think about something you have promised to do in the past but failed to fulfil. Attempt to do it today no matter how long ago the commitment.

DAY 7: SELF CONTROL

Take the day to fast and abstain from something you enjoy. Rather than consume it, take the time to pray gratitude to God.

[13]
SESSION 7:
FOLLOW AND COPY

BIG IDEA

Discipleship is not just about following Jesus; it is also about mimicking His behaviour. The disciples were directed time and time again to do what they saw Jesus doing. This meant, and still means today, that discipleship is about becoming like the teacher. In this session we will think about how to become more like Jesus. How do we follow and how do we copy?

[Q] If you were to be critical of your own faith walk, what are the things you see Jesus do that you struggle to model in your own life?

[Q] Do you ever feel you are a good disciple? Are there times when you feel like a bad disciple? When and what activities make you feel this way?

[Q] What would you like to see in your own life that Jesus did that you have yet to experience?

IMITATION

Modern-day Christianity is so caught up with "church going" that there is a danger we miss the radical life Jesus calls His people to live. As Mother Teresa said in an interview, rather than make it safely to heaven's door, we should hop, skip and jump through life. Don't play it safe. Be playful! The life of a disciple is a disciplined one of following and imitating Jesus. The life of a disciple of Jesus is unique to any other as we learn not only to follow but also to start to do the things He did. Imitation of Jesus is key to actively living out our faith.

PRAYER

Before reading the passage take a moment to pray. Invite the Holy Spirit to speak to the group through the passage. This is key each week. Praying before reading the Bible opens us up to God speaking and shows that we want to learn from Him as well as each other.

Jesus called his twelve disciples to Him and gave them authority to drive out impure spirits and to heal every disease and sickness.

These are the names of the twelve apostles: first, Simon (who is called Peter) and his brother Andrew; James son of Zebedee, and his brother John; Philip and Bartholomew; Thomas and Matthew the tax collector; James son of Alphaeus, and Thaddaeus; Simon the Zealot and Judas Iscariot, who betrayed Him.

These twelve Jesus sent out with the following instructions: "Do not go among the Gentiles or enter any town of the Samaritans. Go rather to the lost sheep of Israel. As you go, proclaim this message: 'The kingdom of heaven has come near.' Heal the sick, raise the dead, cleanse those who have leprosy, drive out demons. Freely you have received; freely give."

[R] MATTHEW 10:1–8

Having read the passage, pause for a moment or two. Some groups may like to read the passage twice – maybe with two different voices or different translations.

Start by facilitating an open discussion on people's reactions to the passage, using questions like:

What jumps out of the passage for you?

Is there anything you struggle with/don't understand?

Are there any new connections you can make within or beyond this passage?

LEARNERS LEARNING

People may ask why Jesus sent the disciples only to the Jews. The disciples were still in the early days of their training. Jesus is sending them out to give what He has been doing a go for themselves. Having shown them how to heal, cast out demons, and teach, He wants them to try out what they have seen Him do with an interested or willing crowd. Later, in the book of Acts, He sends them out to the wider world. The disciples first go to an easy crowd before they are sent to a difficult crowd.

[Q] Jesus sent the disciples out with authority to preach the gospel, heal the sick, and cast out demons. If this was a job description for the life of a disciple, is this what you see happening in the lives of Christians globally today? Where and when have you see this lived out?

[Q] How willing are you to follow Jesus' instructions and do what He did if the opportunity arose? If you are nervous, why is this?

ACTIVITY

WORKSHEET

Ask the group to spend some time on the worksheet on page 64 entitled "Copying Christ".

Step 1: On the left-hand side of the page encourage the group to write the behaviours and activities of Jesus, thinking through what the group remembers about His life, listing His work and character.

Step 2: On the right-hand side of the page spend some time thinking about which of the behaviours and activities of Jesus they would most like to see in their own lives.

Step 3: Invite the participants to explore together, with practical first steps, how they could grow in these things. For example, I could pray for my colleague John who is in hospital addressing healing; I am going to invite my friend Beth to the Alpha group to hear the Good News.

Spend some time reflecting with the group on what activity of Jesus is most appealing to them. Often areas of supernatural ministry and political activism are side-lined for more perceived easier or vague ideas of "being more loving". Challenge the group to explore the healing ministry, prophetic ministry, and a passion for justice issues. All are things that Jesus embodied.

[Q] "Fear of man" is often a reason people give for not giving supernatural ministry a go. What is it about other people and their views that stops you in your tracks?

[Q] Jesus gave the disciples authority to drive out evil spirits. Do you feel like someone with authority? Explore why or why not.

[Q] Ask the group if they have ever realized as a follower of Jesus that they too have authority to heal the sick and do the ministry of Jesus.

FRIGHTENING AND POWERFUL

American Pastor Francis Frangipane once said: "Prayer warriors are the most frightening, powerful demon chasing, world moving beings on earth."

[Q] How do you think your life might be different if you invested in being a disciple who prayed more for healing and the sick… maybe even for the casting out of demons?

FINAL PRAYER

It might be appropriate to end this session by inviting the Holy Spirit and commissioning people to be empowered disciples. If it's appropriate you might like to use this prayer as a way of commissioning and anointing.

COMMISSIONING PRAYER

Father,

Through Your Holy Spirit would You anoint us for Your kingdom ministry. Would You give us authority to heal the sick, passion to lay on hands and pronounce healing.

People of God, Christ invites each of us to faithful discipleship and service. We are all called to different ministries as we seek to live God's love. Jesus wants to commission each of us as His servants to practise His kingdom ministry every single day.

Do you accept the authority Jesus wants to give you?

RESPONSE: *I do.*

Living God, draw us deeper into Your love;

Jesus our Lord, send us to care and serve;

Holy Spirit, make us heralds of the Good News with the authority to announce healing.

Stir us, strengthen us, teach and inspire us to live Your love with generosity and joy, imagination and courage.
May we daily live out the life of Christ in the world today.

Would we follow and copy the life of Christ Jesus.

Amen

WORKSHEET: COPYING CHRIST

The call of a disciple is to follow and copy Christ. Here we explore what Christ is like and how we might see some of His attributes and practices in our own lives.

On the left-hand side of the page write down the behaviours and actions Jesus modelled for the disciples. Think through what you know of His life, listing His work, character and activities. On completion, think about which of these things you would most like to see in your own life. Give yourself practical, manageable, and measurable challenges on the right.

For example: do you want to grow in healing? Perhaps you know someone who is ill you can pray for. Do you want to be a louder voice for justice? Can you join a campaign for a cause you believe is important to Jesus?

JESUS

YOU

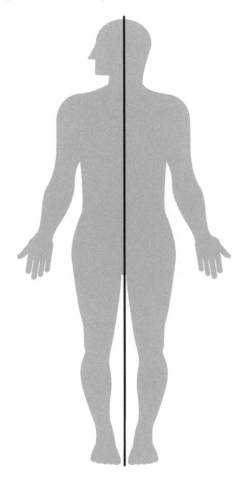

 DOWNLOAD AND PRINT WORKSHEETS AND MORE RESOURCES AT WEAREMAKINGDISCIPLES.COM

TAKE HOME [7] FIND A MENTOR

Think of a mentor like a personal trainer. Without others around us, speaking wisdom and giving clarity we may well find ourselves floundering in our faith.

In a new work place you might be given someone who walks you through your new roll and the company expectations. If you join a course you might have someone who sits with you and supports you as you study and learn. In many walks of life we have these mentors who help direct and support us in new things. A mentor is a wise and trusted counselor or teacher who helps point us in the right direction and models a practice we need to learn:

The Bible gives us numerous examples of mentoring. In Exodus 18 Moses was mentored by his father-in-law, Jethro. In 1 Samuel 1-4 we see the mentoring relationship between Eli and Samuel. Eli prepared Samuel for the tasks and responsibilities that were his after Eli's death. In the gospels we see Jesus mentoring his disciples to lead and minister like Him.

A mentor is there to help and support us in our learning. In some instances, the church has become the focus on Sundays as the place we show people the life of Jesus but in the Bible we see Jesus investing in people every day and every moment. Even a wedding is an opportunity for Jesus to show his disciples what is possible with him.

As you take new steps to grow in faith, spend time with a wiser, discipled Christian who can keep your growth on track. A good mentor, you might call them a spiritual friend, will help answer questions, model a life with Jesus and give you clear direction.

When we become Christians we can have multiple questions, worries and doubts. Having a mentor will give you space to ask questions, talk about your worries and pray for your doubts.

NOTE: Most church leaders cannot personally support everyone that needs mentoring in their community. But every community has elders and seasoned Christians who can speak into your life. Take the opportunity to learn everything and be with someone who can show you everything they can. It's better to learn from those who have done this before than make all the same mistakes other Christians have made.

HOW TO FIND THE RIGHT MENTOR?

Finding the right person with whom you work things through with is key to growing in faith. We encourage you to approach your local church leader or a good Christian friend to help find the right person for you. Tell them you want someone to walk with you in these early days. Take this week to start these conversations to find the right person.

 DOWNLOAD AND PRINT WORKSHEETS AND MORE RESOURCES AT WEAREMAKINGDISCIPLES.COM

[14]
CONCLUSION
THE GREAT COMMISSION

Making Disciples was created to be a platform for reflection and challenge as we seek not just to follow but also copy Rabbi Jesus. From the initial shape tool through the seven-week programme we have intentionally looked at our heads, hearts and hands.

These seven weeks are just the start of the discipleship adventure. We must be willing to learn, see things differently, and be corrected as well as encouraged. We have found that returning to the Discipleship Shape Tool periodically with a mentor or small group helps bed down the changes being made.

As disciples being formed in the likeness of Jesus, we must not only hear what He says but also put it into practice.

The great commission found in both Mark 16 and Matthew 28 gives us a framework for what the mission of a disciple looks like.

He said to them, "Go into all the world and preach the gospel to all creation. Whoever believes and is baptized will be saved but whoever does not believe will be condemned. And these signs will accompany those who believe: in my name they will drive out demons; they will speak in new tongues; they will pick up snakes with their hands; and when they drink deadly poison, it will not hurt them at all; they will place their hands on people who are ill, and they will get well."

[R] MARK 16:15–18 | MY EMPHASIS

Then Jesus came to them and said, "All authority in heaven and on earth has been given to me. Therefore go and make disciples of all nations, baptizing them in the name of the Father and of the Son and of the Holy Spirit, and teaching them to obey everything I have commanded you. And surely I am with you always, to the very end of the age."

[R] MATTHEW 28:18–20 | MY EMPHASIS

Within these two passages Jesus sets out the life of a disciple. Disciples are to **save** the lost, **heal** the sick, **deliver** those imprisoned and make **disciples**.

Jesus says we are to save, heal, drive out, and disciple. He doesn't say memorize what I say on these topics, or learn it in Greek, although memorizing and learning the Greek is helpful. Jesus wants us to actually do this stuff. Imagine Jesus returning and finding that his disciples have in fact not done this but learnt His words verbatim.

THE FOUR COMMANDS OF THE GREAT COMMISSION

GO SAVE

The life of a disciple is a clear one. Jesus wants us to tell people about Him, share His good news, and lead people to salvation through Him. Sometimes we think that it's the travelling missionaries that get to do this wonderful work. But the life of a disciple at the school gate, office block, bus stop or football match takes us to the ends of the earth. It's the role of all followers of Jesus to engage in the life of saving the lost. Jesus promises the disciples at the beginning of the book of Acts that they will go to the ends of the earth, but they will not do it alone. It will be through encountering God that they are empowered for this work.

GO HEAL

Alongside saving the lost, disciples are commissioned to lay hands on and pray for the sick. This is the life of a disciple, not just the super-spiritual few. We are told by Paul in 1 Corinthians 12:8–11 that there are nine gifts of the Spirit, one of which is healing. We are also told in the Scriptures to pray in the name of Jesus (John 14:13), who was the healer. When Jesus commands us to go heal the sick, then we know that it is God's will to see people healed. We aren't twisting God's arm; He is a God who heals and wants to heal. This means His healing power is available to us through His Holy Spirit. We should not be afraid to step out in confidence and pray for healing when it is a genuine need.

The gift of healing is a gift for the whole church. Some people are especially gifted in this area but it doesn't mean that any member of the church cannot see healing miracles at any time. We must remember that some disciples are gifted in this area and some people have simply had more experience, while others have more confidence in seeing the miracle happen. God can use any disciple at any time to reveal His grace to someone in need. The key is to remember that He is the one who heals, while we are the ones who pray for it. This should take the pressure off us and put the pressure on God. With this in mind, we should therefore be free to pray for everyone in need. The more we pray, the more we may see these miracles today.

GO DELIVER

Jesus opened the eyes of His disciples to see the spiritual battle in which they were living. Praying against the work of the evil one, casting out demons, and recognizing the spiritual battle is something that comes with maturity of faith. It is the same for us today.

We need to recognize and remember just how powerful the name of Jesus is. In Mark 16:17 Jesus says, "these signs will accompany those who believe: In my name they will drive out demons; they will speak in new tongues". It's in the name of Jesus that we drive out demons. This area of discipleship should only be matured in a safe environment with others who know how to do this in a healthy way. That being said, we can all pray for those whom we believe the devil is trapping or tricking. We can prayer-walk with power, claiming our streets for Jesus or praying into oppressive places. According to James 5:16, "the prayer of a righteous person is powerful and effective." Our prayers are powerful and effective in earthly realms and heavenly realms. This is the confidence in which we as disciples should walk.

GO DISCIPLE

Once someone is saved, healed, and delivered then our role is to help them grow in faith and know their part in God's plan. This role of discipleship is everyone's and not just the role of the church leader. Matthew 28 tells us to go teach and explain our faith so that people are discipled in Him. It is not possible for only the church leaders to fulfil the discipleship needs of those coming to faith. They can play their part, but it's the responsibility of the whole church to do this. "Go disciple" is the commission to each of us to play our part in the Jesus Movement, handing on the treasure from one generation to the next. This means each disciple should be looking to support and invest in someone else's faith. It's through investing in others that many of us grow the most. This means always looking for opportunities to show people what a life with Jesus looks like. Jesus discipled his followers by opening His life up to them; we must do the same. Discipleship is about allowing people to see how we are growing in faith, putting it into practice, humbly recognising that we sometimes fail and sometimes we see a better way to live. Being a disciple maker is about being open to the lives of others and showing Jesus by example.

As we have worked through this course we have looked at the life of a disciple, allowing our heads, hearts, and hands to become more Christ-like in thought, character, and action. We have seen how our minds need to engage with Scripture, feeding our thoughts. We have considered how to allow space for our hearts to be penetrated by the Spirit so to become hearts of flesh, living passionately for Jesus. And we have explored how our hands actively allow those around us to encounter the good news in action as well as in our lives practising resurrection.

It's through complete discipleship of our heads, hearts, and hands that our entire lives can reflect the God we follow. It's this life of the disciple that hears Jesus' command, understands, and puts into action the great commission to save, heal, deliver, and disciple those around us. The life of a disciple is to go and do what Jesus did and not just memorize His words.

"Therefore go and make disciples of all nations, baptizing them in the name of the Father and of the Son and of the Holy Spirit"

[R] MATTHEW 28:18–20 | MY EMPHASIS

AMEN.

NOTES

_____

_____

_____

_____

_____

_____

_____

_____

_____

_____

_____

_____

[15]
EXTRA SESSION: A HEART THAT IS HEALED

BIG IDEA

As our head begins to understand more of who Jesus is and how it should, in turn, think and perceive the world around it, our heart should also be transformed to a deeper, more intimate love of Jesus and equipped to live a life of mission. However, past hurts, experiences, and failures can mark our hearts and fill us with a sense of failure so that head knowledge cannot penetrate to the depths of who we are. We need a healing encounter with Jesus.

[Q] What experience do you have of failure in your life? How do you react to personal failure?

[Q] Are there previous experiences in life – things you have done or that others have said or done to you – that make it hard for you to fully commit your heart to Jesus?

PRAYER

Before reading the passage take a moment to pray. Invite the Holy Spirit to speak to the group through the passage. This is key each week. Praying before reading the Bible opens us up to God speaking and shows that we want to learn from Him as well as each other.

When they had finished eating, Jesus said to Simon Peter, "Simon son of John, do you love me more than these?"

"Yes, Lord," he said, "you know that I love you."

Jesus said, "Feed my lambs."

Again Jesus said, "Simon son of John, do you love me?"

He answered, "Yes, Lord, you know that I love you."

Jesus said, "Take care of my sheep."

The third time he said to him, "Simon son of John, do you love me?"

Peter was hurt because Jesus asked him the third time, "Do you love me?" He said, "Lord, you know all things; you know that I love you."

Jesus said, "Feed my sheep. Very truly I tell you, when you were younger you dressed yourself and went where you wanted; but when you are old you will stretch out your hands, and someone else will dress you and lead you where you do not want to go." Jesus said this to indicate the kind of death by which Peter would glorify God. Then he said to him, "Follow me!"

[R] JOHN 21:15–19

Having read the passage, pause for a moment or two. Some groups may like to read the passage twice – maybe with two different voices or different translations.

Start by facilitating an open discussion on people's reactions to the passage, using questions like:

What jumps out of the passage for you?

Is there anything you struggle with/don't understand?

Are there any new connections you can make within or beyond this passage?

PASSION

The way a Westerner thinks and behaves can be radically different to that of an Easterner. A Westerner tends to think a lot and is inclined to be less emotional. Westerners tend to keep things emotionally locked down, and Easterners tend to look more expressive, assertive and emotional than Westerners. Jesus was an Easterner who had his emotions fully switched on.

Disciples were expected not only to watch their rabbi but also catch the passion of their rabbi. Jesus talks about this in Revelation 2:4 where He tells the church of Ephesus that they are living out their faith well; they are working hard and not allowing themselves to tolerate wicked behaviour. But Jesus held one thing against them: they had given up their first love. They had lost the fire and passion that they once had. They were living good religious lives but had lost the fire for God in their hearts. A disciple is someone who carries the fire of God within them. The John 21 passage shows Jesus moving and encouraging Peter's heart. Imagine Jesus with a defibrillator trying to restart Peter's heart as He keeps repeating, "Do you love me?" to gain an emotional response from Peter.

[Q] How do you think Peter felt when Jesus sought him out personally to speak to Him?

[Q] In your opinion why does Jesus ask Peter the same question three times?

NOTE: This passage is in the context of Peter's denials of Jesus when He was on trial. If the group are unfamiliar with them you can find this in John 18:15–27.

[Q] Why do you think Jesus does not mention Peter's denials? What does this passage tell us about how Jesus deals with our past failings?

[Q] What is the significance of Jesus' immediate response to Peter each time: "feed/take care of my lambs/sheep"?

[Q] Are there past failures in our lives that might be written over our hearts and prevent us from becoming what Jesus intends for us? How would Jesus deal with these?

[Q] What does loving Jesus really mean? Are there ways of being able to unpack this? Examples or words?

[Q] Before this passage Peter is in the boat hiding; he had run away from the world. Are you hiding from Jesus? Have you ever hidden from Him? How did you feel?

[Q] Peter did something that damaged his relationship with Jesus and this needed to be addressed. Jesus is rectifying Peter's heart. What have you done that Jesus might want you to revisit as a process of practising resurrection on you?

A CHRISTIANITY THAT CAPTURES MY HEART

If your group has time you might like to read and talk about this quote from the late Reverend Robert Capon, the famous New York priest who was also a celebrity chef.

[”]

The most critical issue facing Christians is not abortion, pornography, the disintegration of the family, moral absolutes, MTV, drugs, racism, sexuality, or school prayer. The critical issue today is dullness. We have lost our astonishment.

The Good News is no longer good news, it is okay news. Christianity is no longer life changing, it is life enhancing. Jesus doesn't change people into wild-eyed radicals anymore; He changes them into "nice people."...

What happened to radical Christianity, the un-nice brand of Christianity that turned the world upside-down? What happened to the category-smashing, life-threatening, anti-institutional gospel that spread through the first century like wildfire and was considered (by those in power) dangerous? What happened to the kind of Christians whose hearts were on fire, who had no fear, who spoke the truth no matter what the consequence, who made the world uncomfortable, who were willing to follow Jesus wherever He went?... I'm ready for a Christianity that "ruins" my life, that captures my heart and makes me uncomfortable... I want a faith that is considered "dangerous" by our predictable and monotonous culture.

[R] REVEREND ROBERT CAPON
FROM CHOOSE LIFE: 365 READINGS FOR RADICAL DISCIPLES BY SIMON GUILLEBAUD

FINAL PRAYER

To respond we are going to imagine we are on the beach with Jesus having breakfast. As with Peter, Jesus reminds us of our failures and speaks restoration over them. In this meditation we are going to allow the Holy Spirit to take us back to our places of failure and bring restoration.

Spend a moment allowing the Holy Spirit to present your beach to you. Some of us hate sand – is your beach a pebble beach? Are there other people on the beach with you? What can you hear? As you sit on this beach allow the Holy Spirit to remind you of your past failures.

LEADER: *Jesus says to you, "Do you love me?"*

RESPONSE: *"You know I love You."*

LEADER: *"Go and tell the world I love them.*
        (Pause)
        Do you love me?"

RESPONSE: *"You know I love You."*

LEADER: *"Go and tell your neighbour I love them.*

(Pause) Do you love me?"

RESPONSE: *"You know I love You."*

LEADER: *"Go and tell the broken and hurting I love them. Your past may be defined by fear and failure, but your future is defined by Jesus' forgiveness and God's faithfulness. Father, send us out in the power of your name to live and work to your praise and glory."*

AMEN.

[16]
DETAILS ON THE QUESTIONS

As you are working through the questions used in the Discipleship Shape Tool you may not be clear on what exactly they mean. To help clarify, we have expanded below:

- Under the heading "to what extent are we" you will find more on how to think through your answer to each question.

- Under "can we see" we have offered a suggestion for how you begin moving yourself along the scale towards the centre.

[Q] HOW MUCH IS YOUR DAY-TO-DAY LIFE CHANGING AS YOU THINK ABOUT WHAT IT MEANS TO LIVE FOR JESUS?

To what extent are we:

Letting our knowledge of Jesus change our actions?

Following Jesus in our everyday life?

Can we see:

Ways our actions could align more with Jesus?

[Q] HOW COMMITTED ARE YOU TO A LOCAL CHURCH COMMUNITY?

To what extent are we:

Actively and regularly involved in church, small groups, other forms of community?

Members rather than just spectators in these communities?

Can we see:

Where we could increase our enthusiasm and passion for church and the people in it?

[Q] HOW MUCH WOULD YOU SAY YOUR FAITH LEADS YOU TO LOVE AND CARE FOR OTHERS?

To what extent are we:

Using our time, energy, and resources to love and care for those we encounter who need it?

Actively looking for opportunities to do this?

Can we see:

How God can help us care for even those people we find more difficult to love?

[Q] TO WHAT EXTENT ARE YOU HELPING OTHERS TO SERVE GOD BETTER?

To what extent are we:

Showing others how they can use the gifts God has given them?

Creating space for other people to serve God in different ways?

Can we see:

Anyone in our lives whom we could encourage or enable in the work God has given them to do?

[Q] HOW WILLING ARE YOU TO PUT IN HELPFUL BOUNDARIES?

To what extent are we:

Careful to leave space in our lives for rest so that we are not doing too much and over busy?

(Sometimes low self-esteem leads us to think so low of ourselves we become a doormat. Boundaries protect us from burn-out and stripping of our energy and resources. You are a treasure of God; boundaries will not allow people to trample on the image of God in us.)

Using wisdom to say no to opportunities and people when we feel we need to?

Can we see:

Places in our lives where we are too busy or "in demand" and need to readjust our priorities?

[Q] TO WHAT EXTENT ARE YOU SERVING JESUS IN COLLABORATION WITH OTHERS?

To what extent are we:

Including others in the things we do to serve God?

Willing to share the things we are doing and the things we are excited about?

Can we see:

Anything we are excited about doing at the moment where we could include someone else?

[Q] HOW MUCH ARE YOUR DAILY HABITS CHANGING TO REFLECT GOD'S HEART FOR HIS CREATION?

To what extent are we:

Limiting the negative environmental impact of our choices, such as the energy we use, our transport choices, the rubbish we produce and what we do with it, and the food we eat?

Making ethical choices in the way we shop and live our lives?

Can we see:

Any actions we could take that promote better care for our environment and world?

[Q] HOW MUCH DO TRAGEDY AND INJUSTICE MOVE YOU TO ACTION?

To what extent are we:

Affected when we hear of tragedies in the news and the lives of those in our community?

Moved to do something as a result of this, such as care for someone, sign a petition, write to an MP, take part in protests or actions to change situations?

Can we see:

Where we have been moved by tragedy or injustice and haven't done anything about it yet?

[Q] HOW ENGAGED ARE YOU IN PERSONAL AND COMMUNITY PRAYER LIFE?

To what extent are we:

Having time to regularly pray both on our own and with others?

Actively engaged in these times of prayer?

Can we see:

How God can make us more excited about prayer?

[Q] TO WHAT EXTENT ARE YOU COMPLETELY OPEN AND HONEST ABOUT YOUR STRENGTHS AND FAILURES WITH ONE OR TWO CLOSE FRIENDS?

To what extent are we:

Finding friends with whom we can be honest and support each other in prayer?

Using these friendships to challenge each other to draw closer to Jesus?

Can we see:

Anyone in our lives with whom we could pray and begin to talk through some of these discipleship issues?

[Q] TO WHAT EXTENT ARE AREAS OF SIN AND BROKENESS IN OUR LIVES BEING CHANGED BY JESUS?

To what extent are we:

Seeing things in our life that Jesus wants us to change?

Being proactive in bringing them to God and seeing them changed?

Can we see:

An area that God is currently working on in our lives and anything we can do about this?

[Q] TO WHAT EXTENT IS YOUR RELATIONSHIP WITH GOD BEING REGULARLY CULTIVATED AND DEEPENED?

To what extent are we:

Creating time and space to get to know God better?

Seeing Him change our hearts as we get to know Him better?

Can we see:

A time or place where we could spend some time just to "be" in His presence and let Him draw close to us?

[Q] TO WHAT EXTENT IS YOUR HEART IN LINE WITH GOD'S LOVE AND DESIRES?

To what extent are we:

Growing in our knowledge of what God desires for us and others?

Seeing in the things that inspire, enthuse or challenge us a reflection of how God feels?

Can we see:

A passion or desire in our heart that we think God wants to expand?

[Q] HOW MUCH DO THE BIBLE AND YOUR BELIEFS IMPACT YOUR ATTITUDE TOWARDS CULTURE, THE WORLD AND YOUR COMMUNITY?

To what extent are we:

Thinking through what the Bible has to say about issues we encounter in the news, our workplaces, friendships, families and communities?

Having our attitudes changed by our faith rather than the circumstances we find ourselves in?

Can we see:

A situation in which God might want to use us to speak His wisdom?

[Q] ARE YOU OPEN TO WRESTLING WITH AND BEING CHALLENGED ABOUT THINGS YOU BELIEVE?

To what extent are we:

Willing to embrace questions about faith as a way to grow?

Looking to Jesus in the areas of our faith we find difficult or don't understand?

Can we see:

An area of what we believe where God might want to challenge us or expand our mind further?

[Q] TO WHAT EXTENT ARE YOU ALLOWING YOURSELF TO LEARN FROM THOSE WHO THINK DIFFERENTLY TO YOU?

To what extent are we:

Listening to those we agree with as well as those we disagree with?

Making space in our lives to talk with, listen to sermons by, or read books from people who may have a different perspective on life than ours?

Can we see:

Someone unlike us from whom we may be able to learn something?

[Q] HOW MUCH DO YOU REGULARLY SPEND TIME ENGAGING WITH THE BIBLE?

To what extent are we:

Reading or working through parts of the Bible ourselves?

Engaging with the Bible in other ways, such as through books, podcasts, sermons, small groups or church?

Can we see:

A time in our day when we could regularly read, hear or think about the Bible a little more?

[Q] TO WHAT EXTENT ARE YOU REGULARLY DISCOVERING MORE ABOUT JESUS AND HIS WORK IN OUR WORLD?

To what extent are we:

Growing in our knowledge of who Jesus is?

Learning more about what Jesus has done and wants to do in the world around us?

Can we see:

Something about Jesus that we can learn more about?

[Q] HOW MUCH DO YOU REGULARLY DISCUSS YOUR FAITH WITH OTHERS?

To what extent are we:

Discussing the things we believe and have learnt with others in our church, small groups, etc.?

Talking about God with people who wouldn't call themselves Christians?

Can we see:

Anyone we know with whom we could pray for an opportunity to talk about faith?

[Q] TO WHAT EXTENT DOES YOUR READING OF THE BIBLE POINT YOU TOWARDS JESUS AND HOW TO LIVE FOR HIM?

To what extent are we:

Engaging with the Bible on a deep level so we learn more about Jesus each time we read it?

Seeing from the Bible more about how Jesus wants us to live?

Can we see:

Any ways we could go a little deeper in our interactions with the Bible?

ACKNOWLEGDMENTS

Making Disciples has been shaped by many hands.
Massive thank you to Dan Scott, Colin Shaw, Luke Resch, Rev
Benedict Atkins, Rev Beki Rogers, Alex Hall, and Sara Brayford
for your love of making disciples and partnership in what we do.
Also, big thank you to Peter Martin and Wendy Grisham for your
support and wisdom in bringing this tool to life.